A Certain Style

The Fashionable Dolls of Madame Alexander

Cynthia Gaskill

Gold Horse Publishing

Inquires should be addressed to:
Theriault's Gold Horse Publishing
PO Box 151, Annapolis, Maryland 21404

Art Direction and Design: David W. Hirner
Photography: Vince Lupo

Printed in Hong Kong
ISBN: 0-912823-64-X

Introduction

When you look at a Madame Alexander doll, what do you see? Is it the dazzling outfit created by a top couturier designer with careful attention to every detail and accessory? Is it the worker's hand in the styling of the wig or the attention to sewing detail by expert seamstresses? Or is it, ultimately, the artistry and design of the faces?

Madame Alexander, quite simply, was a visionary. She began a business in a time when women simply didn't do that sort of thing. Starting out small, she always kept the ever-expanding company on the cutting-edge of the industry. In an aggressive marketing strategy, she linked her company with major Hollywood studios in order to promote the latest Alexander celebrity dolls. She also incorporated the sure-fire recipe of favorite childhood and storybook characters as part of her line, using these as a time-tested mainstay while producing some very elaborate and expensive dolls to appeal to an upper echelon of buyers.

She was the first to give dolls personalities and stories to go with their names as is evidenced with the early Alexander company catalogues (which you can be sure she, herself, provided the copy for) lending to them a quality of humanness and warmth that surpassed the fact that this was just another unbreakable doll. It seems only fitting to me that Madame Alexander chose to personify Coco Chanel in the doll she described as "the jewel in the crown" of the company. She and Coco were so very much alike and so ahead of their times. They both had a wonderful head for business as well as an extraordinary sense of design and knowing what people wanted. They were the trend setters of their industries - the movers and shakers, not complacent with the same product and production day after day.

The Madame Alexander dolls within encompass a period of over 50 years. The variations in design, fabrics, and faces, prove what a forward thinker she was as she pushed the doll envelope, so to speak, to constantly provide something new to the public, the industry, and her beloved child admirers. These dolls truly live up to the company motto that "A Doll Made by Madame Alexander is a Gift to Cherish."

To some, curiosity, courage and knowledge come more naturally in collecting and challenge the bounds of normal thinking. Rodney Waller is one such collector. During his long-time membership in the Madame Alexander Doll Club serving as competition judge, lecturer, author and many other positions, he has seen his share of these wonderful creations. His knowledge and leadership in the industry has been an asset to many new collectors and his keen eye for details has kept his, up until now, private collection above par. His attention to notice originality in an undocumented outfit or doll has led him to acquire some rare beauties. Hopefully, he has helped other collectors to find the courage to trust their instincts and knowledge in obtaining these elusive and rare dolls and should indeed be recognized for his contributions within the collecting society.

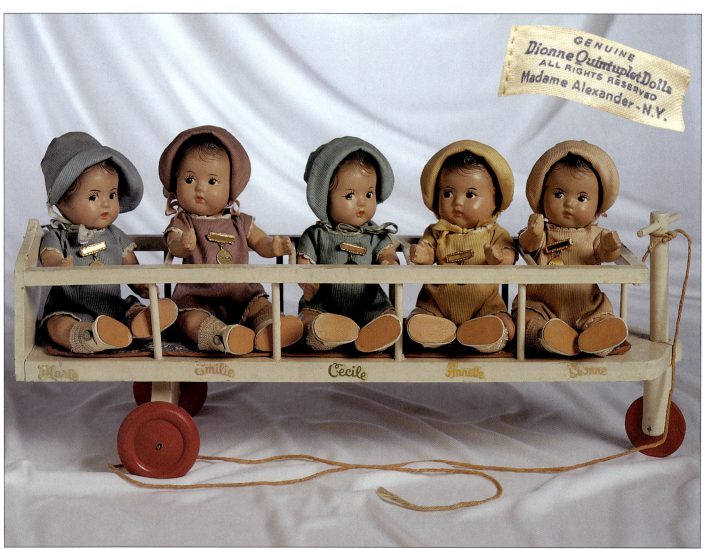

The birth of the Dionne quintuplets in 1935 created a media sensation along with a rash of new advertising opportunities for a chosen few. Only Madame Alexander had the exclusive rights to use the Dionne name on her dolls. They were designed by sculptor Bernard Lipfert who would create many great character dolls to come. All the Dionne sets below are composition, have five-piece bodies marked Alexander, and hand-painted features.

1. Set of Dionne Quintuplets
7 1/2". Set of five babies marked Alexander on head, tagged playsuits with matching sun hats, shoes and socks, and goldtone name pins. Circa 1935. Early edition of the quints with bent legs.

2. Painted Wooden "Quint-o-bile" with Box
18 L. x 6 1/2" H. Painted wooden carrier with three wheels, sectioned seating, and name decals to one side. Circa 1936. Includes rare and original box with label, stamped "43", and penciled price $4.95.

3. Painted Wooden Quint Table and Chairs
Large and round painted wooden table with name decals on table top and five matching side chairs. Circa 1936-37. Hard-to-find accessory has the original Lit Brothers price label of $2.95 on underside.

4. Set of Dionne Toddlers

8". Set of five toddlers marked Dionne Alexander on heads, mohair wigs, painted features, tagged cotton playsuits with matching caps, shoes and socks, and goldtone name pins. Circa 1936. Excellent coloring and painting adds to this complete set.

5. Composition Dr. Dafoe with Wrist Tag

14". Five-piece body with one arm bent, hand-painted features and salt and pepper mohair wig. Tagged cotton pants and attached top, smock having a back tie at neck and matching cap, shoes and socks, and original wrist tag. Circa 1936. Madame Alexander licensed the rights to market a set of the "Little Rascals", however, for some reason they were never put into production. The Dr. Dafoe doll made use of the mold for the character "Spanky" that was never released.

6. Set of Dionne Babies with Nursery Furniture

7 1/2". Early set of quints as babies marked Dionne Alexander on heads with molded hair and bent legs, tagged organdy gowns with matching name bibs, flannel diaper, two have knit booties. Includes painted wooden high chair, crib, playpen, playchair with beads and two scooter chairs. Circa 1936-37. A wonderful, complete set!

The following are a group of early babies and all have cloth bodies, composition heads, hands, bent legs, and sleep eyes.

7. Baby Genius
22". Head marked Alexander, brown eyes and brown mohair wig. Tagged organdy gown with lace and ribbon accents, matching bonnet, cotton slip and pants, booties and socks. Circa 1942-43, #670. Includes original wrist tag and blue ribbon box.

8. Pinkie Baby
18". Head marked Mme Alexander, blue eyes, molded hair. Tagged nylon Christening gown with ribbon and lace accents, matching bonnet, flannel diaper, leatherette booties. Circa 1936. Has original clover wrist tag and blue ribbon box marked #894, wonderfully modelled with fretful expression.

9. Little Genius
16". Head marked Madame Alexander, blue eyes, brown mohair wig. Tagged pink sheer nylon gown with lace and ribbon accents, matching bonnet, slip and panty, leatherette booties. Circa 1942-43. Includes original blue ribbon box with stock #570.

10. Pair of Little Genius Twins
11". Heads marked Mme Alexander, blue tin eyes, molded hair. Tagged organdy gowns with lace and ribbon accents, matching bonnets, pink cotton slip, suedene booties. Circa 1937. This model pre-dates the similar Bitsy and Butch babies.

11. Quiz-Kin
7 1/2". Straight-leg body with yes/no buttons in back to move head, molded hair, polka-dot sunsuit which ties in back, sunhat, shoes and socks. Circa 1953-54.

12. Alexander-kin Baby
7 1/2". Early straight-leg body, molded hair, organdy Christening gown with full slip, flannel diaper and matching bonnet. Circa 1953-54.

13. Quiz-Kin
7 1/2". Straight-leg body with yes/no back buttons to move head, molded hair, tagged blue check sunsuit with lace edging, sun bonnet and tie shoes. Circa 1953-54.

14. Little Shaver
7". Cloth doll with wire armature for bending limbs, pressed mask face with painted features, floss yarn hair. Wears tagged dress of taffeta and organdy with matching slip and panty, black lace mitts, floral bonnet with net, taffeta reticule and black velvet boots (sewn on). Circa 1942-43. Very unusual, smaller size.

15. So-Lite Baby
10". All-cloth baby with molded mask face and elaborately-painted features, yellow looped yarn on head only where the bonnet will show it - the back of the head has a plush covering. Tagged pink organdy gown and matching bonnet with lace accents, slip and flannel diaper, knit booties. Circa 1937. Has original, very plain grey box with label and style #30.

16. Wendy Ann Ice Skater

19". Composition five-piece body, head marked Mme. Alexander, brown sleep eyes, brown braided mohair wig with floral spray. Tagged skating dress of cream damask floral print with red sequin "bows", net shoulder area leading to red satin collar with flowers at shoulders, attached net slip and silk panty with matching lace, cream skates. Circa 1940's. Beautiful model of this doll in a previously undocumented skating outfit.

17. Sonja Henie

15". Composition five-piece body, head marked Madame Alexander/Sonja Henie, brown sleep eyes, open mouth with two teeth, blonde mohair wig with flowers. Tagged white taffeta skating costume with marabou edges, unitard, skates. Circa 1939. Beautifully-costumed version of the international skating star.

18. Sonja Henie Gift Set

15". Composition Sonja Henie doll in wonderfully-preserved presentation trunk which includes skating, skiing, boudoir and casual outdoor outfits as shown, and wearing pink satin party dress with ruffles, matching panty. Circa 1942. Originally featured in many store catalogues, this now hard-to-find set originally sold for $15.

19. Composition Karen Ballerina

15". Five-piece body, head marked Alexander, blue sleep eyes, blonde floss wig with braids wrapped around the head and flowers. Blue net tutu with gold trim, ribbons, flowers and black wristlets, blue nylon panty, tie slippers. Circa 1946. The smallest size of three available with exquisite costume workmanship.

20. Wendy Guardian Angel
8". Straight-leg walker, blonde wig, blue taffeta gown with ribbon bodice and rhinestone accents, silver braid around edges of gown, cotton full slip, nylon panty, gold tie shoes, golden "halo", fabric wings. Circa 1954, #480, came in several gown colors and ribbon styles.

21. Wendy Guardian Angel
8". Straight-leg walker, blonde wig, tagged white taffeta gown with gold trim at hem and sleeves, star brads on front of gown, cotton slip and panty, gold tie shoes, golden "halo" and harp, fabric wings. Circa 1954, #480, in harder-to-find white gown.

22. Maggie Angel
8". Bent-knee walker, reddish wig, bright green eyes, tagged (Maggie) blue taffeta gown with ribbon bodice, silver braid trim at gown edges, panty, silver tie shoes, silver paper wings. Circa 1961, #618, also came in gold-trimmed version.

23. Wendy-Kin Walker
8". Seven-piece walker body, blonde wig, cream party dress with lace trim, satin waist sash with flowers, slip, panty, straw hat with flowers, cream shoes with bows. Circa 1957.

24. Wendy-Kin Walker
8". Seven-piece walker body, blonde wig in pigtails with flowers, black eyes, tagged pink party dress with floral nosegay at waist, slip, panty, basket with chick, magenta shoes. Circa 1957.

25. Alexander-kin Groom
8". Bent-knee walker, auburn short wig, suedene tail-coat with boutonniere, cream shirt, grey cravat with rhinestone, tan cummerbund, pinstripe pants, black shoes and socks. Circa 1957, #377.

26. Wendy Bride
8". Bent-knee walker, brunette wig, tagged tulle, satin ribbon and lace gown with attached full slip, panty, veil with cap style headpiece, cream satin shoes with center rhinestone, garter, bouquet. Circa 1961, #480.

27. Wendy Bridesmaid
8". Straight-leg walker, blonde wig, tagged pink organdy and tulle gown with floral garland, panty, floral headpiece and cream shoes with pink tie. Circa 1955, #478.

28. Wendy Flower Girl
8". Bent-knee walker, brunette wig, tagged pleated blue organdy gown with lace accents, satin sash, separate slip and panty, floral coronet, cream shoes with rhinestones. Circa 1959, #445, Wendy in Flowergirl Outfit.

29. Wendy Dressed For a June Wedding
8". Straight-leg body, blonde wig, tagged pink taffeta dress with layers of pin-tucks, flower accent, long slip, panty, pink hat with tucked back and flowers, gold tie shoes. Circa 1956, #605.

30. Princess Margaret Rose
18". Five-piece body, blue sleep eyes, light-brown curled mohair wig, head marked Alexander. Tagged lavender organdy gown with open dot pattern, diamond lace edging, pink rayon slip and panty, bead necklace, net hose, cream shoes and flower at shoulder, floral garland in hair. Circa 1950. Many styles of gowns were created by Madame Alexander for Princess Margaret Rose, though she usually had blonde hair.

31. Princess Margaret Rose
14". Five-piece body, green sleep eyes, blonde curled mohair wig. Tagged lavender gown as described for #30 but with lace variation at hips and sleeves, pink rayon slip, panty, net hose, cream shoes, flowers at shoulder and in hair, bouquet. Circa 1950, with original clover wrist tag.

32. Nina Ballerina
18". Five-piece body, blue sleep eyes, blonde floss wig curled atop head. Tagged elaborate white tutu of stain and pleated organdy with floral and silver trim accents, attached stiff underskirt and separate slip attached to panty, bead necklace, pink slippers. Circa 1949. Beautiful coloring, original clover leaf wrist tag.

33. Sally Bride
19". Five-piece composition body, blue sleep eyes, brunette mohair wig. Tagged organdy gown with lace hem and floral accents, attached cotton underliner, pants, long lace and net veil, cream shoes and bouquet. Circa 1938.

34. Wendy Bridesmaid
15". Five-piece composition body, blue sleep eyes, blonde mohair wig, head marked Mme Alexander. Tagged pink satin gown with matching bows and trim accents, attached slip, panty, cream tie shoes, matching muff. Circa early 1940's.

35. Babs Skating
18". Five-piece body, head marked
Alexander, blue sleep eyes, honey-blonde,
curled mohair wig. Tagged pink satin skating outfit with marabou trim, matching bonnet, pink slip and panty, golden skates.
Circa 1950. Exceptional coloring and hand-
painting of features, original clover wrist tag.

36. Wendy-Kin Walker
8". Bent-knee walker, auburn wig, tagged pink organdy pleated dress with flowers at waist, lace accents, pink slip and panty, straw hat with flowers, pink shoes. Circa 1958, #571, Wendy Dressed in Another Party Dress.

37. Wendy-Kin Walker
8". Bent-knee walker, blonde wig, tagged (Wendy-Kin) pink organdy dress with dotted bodice and silk flower, matching bonnet, slip and panty, black shoes. Circa 1957-58, though similar to an earlier fashion without the silk flowers.

38. Wendy-Kin Walker
8". Bent-knee walker, blonde wig, tagged white organdy dress with lace and trim accents, pink waist ribbon, slip, panty, black hat with flowers, carries basket with matching flowers, black shoes. Circa 1957.

39. Wendy Goes to the Matinee
8". Straight-leg walker, brunette wig, white taffeta dress with lace accents, matching panty, pink gabardine coat with capelet collar, felt bonnet with flowers, black shoes. Circa 1955, #463, bonnet variation.

40. Wendy-Ann Walker
8". Straight-leg walker, auburn wig, pink organdy dress with bodice pintucks, flowers and ribbon at waist, slip, panty, hat with flowers, blue shoes. Circa 1956.

41. Billy Looks So Spic and Span
8". Bent-knee walker, short brunette wig, blue cotton suit with attached white shirt, matching cap, shoes. Circa 1958, #567.

42. Graduation Wendy
8". Bent-knee walker, blonde wig pulled back over top of head, tagged dotted organdy long dress with lace tiers, waist ribbon, full slip, panty and cream shoes. Circa 1957, #399.

43. Wendy-Kin Walker with Box
8". Straight-leg walker, blonde wig, panty, socks and black shoes. Circa 1955, #400, Basic Wendy with box and booklet.

44. Maggie Mixup with Box
8". Bent-knee walker, reddish wig, bright green eyes, panty, socks and shoes. Circa 1961, #600, Maggie Mixup with original box and booklet.

45. Wendy-Kin Walker with Box
8". Bent-knee walker, blonde wig, striped panty, socks and cream shoes. Circa 1961, #400, Basic Wendy with original box and booklet.

46. Fairy Queen
18". Five-piece body, blue sleep eyes, dark blonde mohair wig, head marked Alexander. Tagged gown of cream net with gold trim and accents, flowers at various areas on dress, attached long slip, panty, hose, cream shoes with bow, mesh wings and golden crown. Circa 1947. Lovely facial painting of this model with original clover wrist tag.

46A. Good Fairy
14". Five-piece body, blue sleep eyes, blonde mohair wig, head marked Alex. Tagged gown of cream taffeta with gold trim and accents, turquoise bead at neckline, long pink slip and panty, hose and shoes, mesh wings and golden crown. Circa 1948. Includes the hard to find, original "magic wand".

47. Set of Lissy Little Women
12" each. Five-piece bodies, assorted eyes and wig colors. Six characters from the book includes Marme, Jo, Beth, Amy, Meg and Laurie in tagged outfits as shown. Circa 1960, #1125 for Little Women and 1967, #1226 for Laurie. A desirable set with excellent coloring.

48. Cinderella
8". Straight-leg walker, blonde wig, blue taffeta gown with rhinestone and star accents, silver trim, side panniers, long slip with net, panty, silver slippers and crown. Circa 1955, #492 with unusual taffeta version of normally a satin gown.

49. Sleeping Beauty
10". Five-piece adult body marked Mme Alexander but with flat feet, blue sleep eyes, blonde wig. Tagged aqua taffeta gown with gold net bodice and sleeve overlay, slip, panty, blue slippers, gold net cape, golden crown with rhinestones. Circa 1959, a special limited edition doll made for Disneyland and sold one year only.

50. Alice In Wonderland
8". Straight-leg body, blonde wig with blue ribbon, tagged dress of blue cotton with white cotton pinafore, slip, bloomers, hose and shoes. Circa 1972-1977, #452 with the original Walt Disney World price sticker, box and wrist tag.

51. Snow White
8". Straight-leg body, brunette wig with white ribbon, tagged gown of blue velvet top attached to gold taffeta skirt, long slip, pantyhose, panty, scarlet rayon cape with silver net collar. Circa 1972-77, #455 with original box and wrist tag.

52. Alexander-Kin Character
8". Straight-leg walker body, blonde wig, black felt overall outfit with red trim and felt flowers, matching short jacket and hat, striped stockings and black shoes. Circa 1955. Unusual outfit, possibly Alexander though untagged, similar in styling to previous storybook "Hansel".

53. Prince Charming

18". Five-piece body, green sleep eyes, red caracul wig, head marked Alexander. Tagged cream brocade jacket with metallic gold trim, matching satin-lined cape, feathered cap, tights, gold ribbon garter, cream shoes. Circa 1950, with fresh coloring.

54. Cinderella

18". Five-piece body, blue sleep eyes, blonde floss wig. Tagged blue satin gown with silver metallic trim, silver star studs, side panniers, long slip and matching panty, hose, golden braid crown, gold mesh snood, beaded bracelet and necklace, clear "glass" slippers. Circa 1950, #8800 in original box with clover "Cinderella" wrist tag and price tag of $13.95 from The Fair store in Chicago.

The following three gift sets show how far ahead of the industry Madame Alexander stood. As early as 1961 she was using a little-known, two-part adhesive item called velcro that allowed for changing of wigs on the doll's heads. It seemed the rest of the world didn't see the value of its every-day use for another 20 or so years. These sets are extremely hard to find intact and unplayed with.

55. Pamela Gift Carrying Valise

12". Five-piece body, blue sleep eyes, head is bald and has an ingenious strip of velcro for attachment of wigs. Comes with various costumes, accessories and three saran wigs. Circa 1963. A hard-to-find presentation piece, #1290.

56. Pamela Gift Set

12". Five-piece body, blue sleep eyes, head is bald for different wig placement. Contains an eight-piece trousseau, two wigs, comb and hairpins in a frame-view gift box. Circa 1963, #1280. Another hard-to-find presentation set with rare, original outer sleeve (Marshall Field price tag).

57. Cissette Trousseau

10". Seven-piece body, sleep eyes, bald head with velcro strip to change wigs. Contains a ten-piece trousseau of clothes, accessories and three saran wigs in a frame-view gift box. Circa 1961, #790.

58. Easter Presentation Egg
Contains an 8" doll with bent-knee body, yellow cotton playsuit, shoes, two extra outfits and wrist tag in a German paper mache egg. Circa 1966. A lovely example of this hard-to-find specialty item.

59. Wendy Sewing Basket
Contains an 8" doll with bent-knee body, yellow cotton playsuit, shoes. Comes with pre-cut outfits to be sewn by hand for Wendy. Circa 1966-69. An FAO Schwarz exclusive.

60. Glamour Set
A lavish set for doll's beauty includes hair accessories, brush, comb, curlers, ribbons, mirror, flowers and hair pieces, boudoir set and hair cream and lotion containers with directions. Circa 1951, FAO Schwarz. Box end reads "6 Blonde".

61. Margaret O'Brien Babs Skater
14". Five-piece body, brunette mohair wig with side braid loops, sleep eyes, head marked Alex. Tagged (Babs Skating) blue satin skating outfit with marabou trim, matching bonnet, nylon slip with attached panty, gold skates. Circa late 1940's. Rare and unusual combination of Margaret O'Brien as a skater with clover wrist tag (Babs) in original box marked #5140.

62. Rare Pair of Composition Wendy Anns in Provincial Costumes
13″ each. Six-piece composition bodies with swivel waist marked Wendy Ann/Mme Alexander/New York, brunette human hair wigs, sleep eyes.
Both wear elaborately-detailed ethnic costumes representative of traditional folk costumes of Hungary. Alexander lace, stitching and detail can all be
noted on these costumes but they are untagged and no further documentation exists as to what they might have been made for. Circa 1940's. Were
they early prototypes for what would be her most popular and longest-lasting series of nationality dolls, or were they a specially-commissioned pair?
These dolls were featured in 1990 in an article from the Winter Newsletter of the Madame Alexander Doll Club. They remain a mystery.

64. Little Southern Girl
8". Straight-leg body, auburn wig, tagged organdy dress with lace accents, tulle puffed sleeves, matching bonnet with flowers, pink taffeta slip with blue ribbon and matching pantaloons, blue shoes. Circa 1953-54.

65. Wendy Invites a Guest for Luncheon
8". Bent-knee walker body, brunette wig with pink ribbon, black eyes, tagged organdy dress with tucks and portrait collar, ribbon sash, slip and panty, black shoes. Circa 1956, #542.

66. Maypole Dance Wendy-Kin Walker with Box
8". Straight-leg walker body, brunette wig, blue sleep eyes, tagged pink organdy dress with blue organdy pinafore and lace accents, pink straw hat, slip, panty, shoes. Circa 1954, with box labelled #522 and wrist tag.

67. Wendy Off To Play
8". Straight-leg walker body, brunette wig, sleep eyes, tagged pink swiss dot dress with lace accents, pink ribbon, straw hat with flowers, slip, panty, shoes. Circa 1957, #401 variation.

68. Little Victoria
8". Straight-leg body, auburn wig, tagged dress of black velvet bodice with puff sleeves, striped polished cotton skirt with complimentary trim, long organdy slip, panty, black shoes, straw hat with flowers. Circa 1954, #328.

69. Wendy-Kin in School Dress
8". Straight-leg walker body, brunette wig, tagged pink dress with floral print, rickrack trim, matching bloomers, black shoes, hat with flowers, holds basket of flowers. Circa 1956, school dress.

70. Wendy Takes a Basket of Fruit to Grandma's
8". Bent-knee walker body, brunette wig with special rolled hairdo, floral print dress, green pinafore-style front attached, matching bloomers, cream shoes. Circa 1956, #566.

71. Wendy-Kin in School Dress
8". Straight-leg walker, brunette wig, tagged green cotton dress with floral print pinafore, matching bloomer, black shoes, green straw hat with pink ribbon. Circa 1955, #444 School Dress.

72. Scarlett
8". Bent-knee walker body, brunette wig with special pulled-back hairstyle atop head, black sleep eyes. Formal rosebud muslin dress with lace accents, green tulle parasol, cotton long full slip and pantaloons, milan straw hat with flowers and long velvet ribbons, black shoes. Circa 1956, #631, a hard-to-find fashion.

73. Scarlett
8". Bent-knee walker body, blonde wig with special pulled-back hairstyle atop head, sleep eyes. Tagged white organdy tiered gown with ribbons and ruffles, red "jewel" at bodice, taffeta long slip and pantaloons, red shoes, straw hat with flowers and tulle bow. Circa 1957, #431, a hard to find and very unusual variation as she has blonde hair.

74. Cissy Scarlett

18". Seven-piece adult body, brunette-styled wig, blue/green sleep eyes. Tagged (Cissy) elaborate and full gown of sheerest organdy with ribbon inserts, lace accents and neckline, hoop underskirt, panty, hose green heels, cameo, pearl necklace, pearl drop earrings, gloves and large horsehair picture hat with flowers. Circa 1958, reported to be one in a series of only 12 made this year, and previously not photographed.

The following dolls are a part of the Godey Series from 1950. All have five-piece hard plastic bodies with sleep eyes. The women have Margaret faces, the man has a Maggie face. They are all very elaborately costumed in beautiful fabrics and have incredible costume detail thus limiting their production.

75. Godey Man/Groom
Blonde floss wig styled into mutton chops on sides. Tagged outfit includes black tuxedo tails jacket, satin shirt attached to cummerbund and pants with side stripe, black shoes and socks, boutonniere and shell watch fob. Has the original clover wrist tag and labelled box bottom.

76. Godey Bride
Blonde floss wig with rolled curls atop head. Tagged satin wedding gown with lace-accented panniers, center rose, elaborate bustle-back leading into train, veil with lace ruffles framing face and tying at chin, long cotton petticoat, matching long bloomers with blue bows, rayon hose, cream snap shoes. Tag reads "Godey Lady".

77. Godey Lady
Light-brown floss wig pulled back into a snood, bangs. Tagged "Godey Lady" pink taffeta dress with double panniers, white satin front, unusual floss edging, matching bonnet with lace, floral and feather plume accents, black velvet tie and reticule, long pink petticoat, matching bloomers, rayon hose, black bow side-snap shoes. Original clover wrist tag.

78. Godey Lady
Light-brown floss wig rolled into side buns with ribbons. Tagged "Godey Lady" gold taffeta gown with ruffled overskirt, open lace accents and ruffled organdy sleeve insets, flowers at waist, long white cotton petticoat with matching pantaloons, rayon hose, black bow side-snap shoes, metal flower charm necklace (the same charm is found on some skirts for Pamela). Original clover wrist tag and box bottom marked "Godey #1843".

79. Godey Lady
Light-brown floss wig pulled back on sides into a snood. Tagged "Godey Lady" peach taffeta gown edged with black lace, apron front with back double bustlet, green velvet top with gold and black trim, matching trim on green felt bonnet with lace and plume, pink cotton long petticoat with matching pantaloons, rayon hose and black bow side-snap shoes. Original clover wrist tag.

Portrettes

"Madame Alexander inspired by the many requests for 11" reproductions of her famous annual collection of Portrait Dolls designed in, exacting detail, this group of dolls" was the description in the 1968 catalogue for these smaller beauties, all having a Cissette body. They were produced this first year in maroon and gold "picture frame" boxes and have wrist tags.

80. Godey
Auburn wig, tagged pink taffeta and ecru lace ruffled dress.

81. Scarlett
Brunette wig, tagged green taffeta gown with black trim.

82. Renoir
Brunette wig, tagged navy taffeta dress with large red picture hat.

83. Agatha
Brunette wig, tagged red velvet dress with lace accents.

84. Southern Belle
Blonde wig, white organdy gown with lace and green ribbon trim.

85. Melinda
Blonde wig, turquoise taffeta gown with lace accents.

86. Gainsborough Cissette
10". Tosca wig, tagged pale blue taffeta gown with velvet waist ribbon, floral accents at shoulders, long slip, panty, hose, matching picture hat, earrings, silver heels. Circa 1957, #961, with Cissette box.

87. Cissette Formal
10". Auburn wig, tagged lime green satin gown with scalloped hem and floral accents, tulle portrait collar and gown bottom, attached slip, pearl earrings, gold heels. Circa 1961, #830, with lace teddy beneath gown.

88. Jacqueline
10". Brunette wig with spit curl, blue eye-shadow and painted lashes, mauve lips. Tagged blue satin gown with sequin trim and attached (by snaps) stole with fringed hem-line, hose, panty, earrings, "diamond" ring, heels. Circa 1962, #886, with Jacqueline box and extra pair of black heels.

89. Cissette Formal
10". Blonde wig with flowers to one side, tagged peach taffeta gown with tulle overlay, large folded sash at waist side with flowers, hose, pearl earrings, gold heels. Circa 1961, an exclusive for FAO Schwarz.

90. Quiz-Kin Groom
7 1/2". Five-piece body, molded hair, black felt tailcoat with boutonniere over one-piece shirt and grey flannel pants with suedene vest, satin cravat and rhinestone tac, black socks and shoes. Circa 1953.

91. Wendy-Ann Bride
7 1/2". Five-piece body, blonde wig, tagged bridal gown of satin and tulle, attached slip, organdy panty, bonnet of lace with attached veil and flowers, bridal bouquet, cream slippers with rhinestones. Circa 1953.

92. Wendy Bridesmaid
8". Five-piece walker body, blonde wig, tagged pink organdy gown with tulle overlay, flowers at waist, panty, horsehair picture hat, pink satin tie slippers. Circa 1955, #478, with hat variation.

93. Wendy Wears a Bridesmaid Dress
8". Seven-piece walker body, brunette wig, tagged organdy gown with stitched floral accents, taffeta slip and panty, picture hat with flowers, cream shoes. Circa 1958, #583.

94. Wendy's First Long Dancing Dress
8". Seven-piece walker body, auburn wig in special side-part top-curled hairdo and tied with green velvet ribbon. Tagged tulle gown with ribbon flower accents, velvet waist sash, satin tie slippers. Circa 1956, #606.

95. Groom
18". Five-piece body, Margaret head marked Alexander, red caracul wig. Black gabardine tuxedo with tails, cotton pique shirt and cummerbund, white bow tie, rhinestone tac, boutonniere, pocket watch chain, black felt top hat, socks and shoes. Circa 1950-54, with original clover wrist tag.

96. Peggy Bride
18". Five-piece body, Margaret head marked Alexander, red mohair wig. Tagged bridal gown of silk georgette with attached taffeta slip, panty, hose, blue garter, cream slippers, tulle veil attached to floral accented bandeau, bridal bouquet. Circa 1950, with original clover wrist tag.

97. Cissy Formal
18". Nine-piece hard plastic body with vinyl arms, styled brunette wig. Tagged pink satin gown with flowers at bodice, Orlon stole, pink slip, panty, cocktail ring, silver heels. Circa 1956.

98. Cissy
18". Nine-piece hard plastic body with vinyl arms, styled blonde wig. Tagged lace teddy, panty, hose, pearl earrings, hairbow, pink heels with flowers. Circa 1954.

99. Rare Cissy Formal

18". Seven-piece hard plastic body (vinyl one-piece arms), head marked Alexander, highly-styled auburn wig with purple velvet bow, blue sleep eyes with exaggerated diagonally-cut lashes. Tagged lilac layered tulle gown with floral cascades and shoulder bouquets, double layer slip, panty, hose, mauve mitts, "diamond" circlet earrings, amethyst ring, lilac heels, original wrist booklet.

The diagonally-cut lashes, dress style, and color palette are strikingly familiar of the Arlene Dahl portrait from 1951 and yet similar exaggerated lashes are found on the Portraits with Cissy faces from 1961. There is no documentation of this outfit ever having gone into production but an Alexander archive photograph does show a series of portrait dolls with the Cissy face and elaborate outfits. This rare doll has exceptional coloring and appears to be one-of-a-kind but remains a mystery as to who she is and what she was created for.

100. Wendy Loves to Waltz
8". Five-piece walker body, blonde wig with top pulled to the back of head, hair bow, tagged white organdy ruffled gown with red rickrack trim, waist sash, slip, panty, red tie slippers and reticule. Circa 1955, #476.

101. Tea Party at Grandma's
8". Five-piece walker body, blonde wig, tagged organdy dress with red rickrack trim, slip, panty, straw hat with red berries, red shoes. Circa 1955, #447.

102. Wendy Ann Walker
8". Seven-piece walker body, blonde wig in special hairstyle with black hairbow, tagged pleated navy cotton dress, double tulle slip, panty, black shoes. Circa 1956.

103. Billy Walker
8". Seven-piece walker body, blonde side-part wig, tagged white shirt, blue shorts with matching cap, tie shoes, and carries a camera. Circa 1956.

104. Wendy Wearing an Outfit for a Plane Trip
8". Five-piece walker body, blonde wig, tagged white cotton dress, navy felt jacket with white collar, matching beanie with pompoms, panty, black shoes. Circa 1955, #452.

105. Wendy Does the Highland Fling
8". Five-piece walker body, brunette wig, tagged red dress with tartan sash and matching tam with plume, long organdy slip, panty, black shoes. Circa 1955, #484.

106. Wendy-Kin Walker
8". Five-piece walker body, auburn wig, tagged red taffeta dress with matching panty, organdy pinafore, black shoes. Circa 1955.

107. Wendy-Kin Walker
8". Seven-piece walker body, tosca wig, tagged red stripe day dress, panty, and red straw hat. Circa 1956.

108. Wendy-kin Walker
8". Seven-piece walker body, bright green eyes, blonde wig in special side curls, organdy dress with lace accents, apron, ruffled panty, straw hat, red shoes. Circa 1953 outfit.

109. Little Men Nat
15". Five-piece body, Maggie head, brown short wig. Tagged "Nat" shirt with attached panty, blue pants with black waist band and elastic braces, satin bow tie, yellow felt jacket and cap, black socks, tan shoes. Circa 1952, #1501, having exceptional coloring.

110. Little Men Tommy Bangs
15". Five-piece body, Margaret head, blonde short hair. Tagged "Tommy Bangs" shirt with attached panty, green pants with green waist band, elastic braces, satin knotted tie, green felt jacket and cap, black socks, grey shoes. Circa 1952, #1501, having exceptional coloring.

Note - All three Little Men came only in the 15" size and had only one style number.

111. Set of Little Women
15". Five-piece hard plastic bodies, styled floss wigs, tagged outfits include dresses with wonderful detail, full-length cotton slip and pantaloons, black bow shoes. Circa 1948-49, #1500. Extraordinary set of four sisters from the Alcott novel, all having original clover wrist tags and original boxes. Original, fresh coloring is a highlight of this award-winning set with the outfits having various detail making each one a special creation.

112. Scarlett O'Hara
11". Composition five-piece body, black styled wig, green eyes. Tagged "Scarlett O'Hara" dress of red velvet bodice, red stripe cuffs and skirt with attached cotton hoop skirt, lace at neckline, matching velvet bonnet with plume, pantaloons with ribbon insert, red shoes. Circa 1940. Always desirable Scarlett in a hard-to-find outfit with original picture wrist tag.

113. Spanish Boy
9". Five-piece composition body marked Mme Alexander New York, black mohair wig, painted features. Tagged "Spanish" outfit of cotton shirt with tie, attached black felt pants with trim, satin waist sash, straw hat with trim, black shoes, wooden castanets. Circa 1937, the forerunner to the widely popular nationality series of today.

114. Little Betty
7". Five-piece composition body marked Mme Alexander, light-brown mohair wig with flowers to the side, painted features, shoes and socks. Dress is organdy with lace and satin sash, teddy and slip. Circa 1935. The clothing is sewn together on the doll and is probably one of the Dolls of the Month series.

115. Composition W.A.A.C.
14". Composition five-piece body, blonde mohair wig, tagged uniform of olive shirt and tie with attached brown skirt, jacket and matching cap, slip and panty, brown shoulder satchel (with V for Victory on flap) and shoes. Circa 1942, part of a series of war-time dolls which included a W.A.V.E., W.A.A.F., Soldier, Marine and Miss America.

116. Margot Ballerina
18". Five-piece body, Maggie head, brown floss wig styled in snood, tagged yellow tutu with taffeta bodice, layered organdy skirt with flowers, matching taffeta panty with gold trim, pink slippers, black velvet choker. Circa 1951, unusual color variation of this outfit.

117. Margot Ballerina
18". Five-piece body, Maggie head, brown floss wig in snood with floral crown, tagged red tutu with taffeta bodice, layered net skirt with flowers, matching satin panty with gold trim, red slippers, velvet choker. Circa 1951, with original clover wrist tag.

118. Parlour Maid
8". Seven-piece walker body, tosca wig, tagged black taffeta dress with white organdy cuffs and apron, slip, panty, lace cap, black shoes. Circa 1956, #579.

119. Southern Belle
8". Seven-piece walker body, blonde wig in special side-curl style, turquoise striped taffeta gown with elaborate styling, back bustle and train, petti-coat, bloomers, straw hat with flowers, brilliant earrings, black shoes. Circa 1956, with ear-ring variation.

120. Little Women Marme
8". Seven-piece walker body, brunette wig in special style, tagged black and white taffeta dress with organdy fichu, chintz apron, petticoat, pan-taloons and black shoes. Circa 1958, #581.

121. Little Women Beth
8". Seven-piece walker body, brunette wig pulled atop head, tagged chartreuse taffeta dress with floral-print pinafore, petti-coat, pantaloons, black shoes. Circa 1956, #609.

122. Little Madaline
8". Five-piece body, blonde wig, pink polka dot dress with lace and ribbon accents, tulle lower sleeves, slip, pantaloons, straw bonnet with flowers, cream shoes. Circa 1953, with hat variation from usual bonnet.

123. Baby Clown
8". Five-piece walker body, red plush wig, painted clown make-up on face, black eyes. Two-tone taffeta suit with gold and floral trims, green felt hat with flowers, tulle neck ruff, gold slippers. Circa 1955, #464, with leashed dog "Huggy".

124. Wendy Goes to a Birthday Party
8". Five-piece walker body, blonde wig, tagged mauve taffeta dress with organdy pinafore trimmed with flowers, panty, straw hat with flowers, black shoes. Circa 1955, #455.

125. Wendy Goes Marketing
8". Five-piece walker body, blonde wig in braids, tagged dress with pink checked cotton and pique, matching panty, purse and black shoes. Circa 1955, #423.

126. Marcella
20". Composition five-piece body, blonde mohair wig, brown eyes, open mouth. Tagged peach organdy dress with openwork crochet collar with flowers, matching straw bonnet with ruffled peach organdy lining, one-piece slip with panty, cream shoes with bows. Circa 1936. Hard-to-find early doll similar to the Little Colonel model.

127. McGuffey Ana
14". Five-piece composition body, blonde mohair wig with front curls and braids, blue eyes, open mouth. Tagged dress of yellow organdy with peach pinafore having lace accents, matching bonnet, one-piece slip and panty, black shoes. Circa 1937. A standard, favorite character of Alexander's.

127A. Princess Elizabeth
13". Five-piece composition body with Betty face, blonde human hair wig, blue decal eyes. Tagged pale blue taffeta gown with floral accents, matching reticule, slip with attached panty, silver crown, silver shoes. Circa 1937, portrays the Princess at the time of her father's coronation. Only this first year was the Betty face used as a special mold was made for 1938 and used thereafter.

128. Rare Judy Portrait with Original Box and Wrist Tag

21". Five-piece composition body, Wendy-Ann face with hand-painted eyebrows, smoky blue shadow and liner, eyelashes, full red lips and nails, brown mohair wig in elaborate coiffure with flowers throughout. Tagged formal gown of lilac taffeta with pink taffeta pinch pleats and inserts, flowers at bodice and front hem, tulle neck insert with satin ribbon finish, unusual zipper dress back, pink cotton full slip with lace hem and matching panty, pink tie slippers and bouquet of flowers with ribbons. Circa 1946.

Madame Alexander
New York U.S.A.

One of 12 portraits created this year with exhibition-quality gowns and outfits. This one supposedly portrayed Judy Garland in the film "Meet Me in St. Louis". It has the original price tag from The Rike Kumeer Company marked $75.00 attached to the slip. Original clover wrist tag and brown oversized box (with early office and factory address at 153 E 24th St NY) within larger shipping box.

129. Lady Churchill
18". Five-piece walker body with Margaret face, blonde styled wig, brown eyes. Tagged pink satin gown, matching opera coat with rhinestones circling neckline, pink slip with hoop, matching panty, hose, cream slippers, brilliant earrings (glued), metal tiara, satin purse. Circa 1953, a companion for the Beaux Art Creation of Queen Elizabeth.

130. Estrella
18". Five-piece walker body with Maggie face, auburn styled wig, blue eyes. Tagged pale lilac gown with elaborate trims and metal floral studs, net sleeves, salmon sash with long back, slip with hoop, panty, hose, mitts, jeweled necklace and tiara, pink tie slippers. Circa 1953, another coronation companion.

131. Maggie Mixup
8". Seven-piece walker body, red wig, freckles, tagged (Maggie) gingham dress with white collar, slip, panty, hat with flower, white shoes. Circa 1961, #617, "Maggie's Favorite School Dress".

132. Maggie with Box
8". Seven-piece walker body, red wig in shorter than normal cut and curled, freckles, red chintz dress with bow and rickrack trim, eyelet slip, bloomer-style red panty, straw hat with rose, black shoes. Circa 1960, unidentified outfit in box faintly-labelled #551.

133. Wendy Walker
8". Seven-piece walker body, blonde wig, blue gingham dress with wide lace-trimmed collar, panty, white shoes. Circa 1959, sold as a boxed outfit but also came on doll.

134. Bill Walker
8". Seven-piece walker body, tagged shirt and attached shorts, red trim at waist, bowtie, red jacket, cream tie shoes. Circa 1963.

135. Wendy Walker
8". Seven-piece walker body, tagged white and blue dress with red waist trim, bowtie, red jacket, black shoes. Circa 1963, a companion doll for the previous.

136. Wendy Ready For Any Weather
8". Seven-piece walker body, blonde wig in long, curled pigtails, gold taffeta raincoat and hat, floral print dress with matching panty, black boots. Circa 1956, #572.

137. Maggie in Rain Wear
8". Seven-piece walker body, red hair, freckles, tagged blue taffeta rain coat with matching hat, light-blue taffeta dress underneath, panty, black shoes. Circa 1956, extra boxed outfit on later Maggie model.

138. Wendy Ready For Any Weather
8". Seven-piece walker body, blonde wig, gold taffeta rain coat and hat, floral print dress with matching panty, tan boots. Circa 1956, #572.

139. Wendy-Kin Walker
8". Seven-piece walker body, blonde wig, navy striped dress with lace, slip, panty, red straw hat, red shoes and toy. Circa 1957.

140. Wendy Off to School
8". Seven-piece walker body, blonde wig in braids, tagged red striped dress with blue pinafore, matching panty, red straw hat, black shoes. Circa 1958, #570.

141. Wendy Cowgirl
8". Seven-piece body, blonde wig, tagged "Cow Girl" outfit of white shirt with attached tan suedene skirt and matching vest with felt flowers and trim, panty, brown boots with red stars, felt hat. Circa 1966, #724.

142. Cowboy Billy
8". Seven-piece body, brunette wig, tagged "Cow Boy" outfit of white shirt with attached brown suedene pants, bolo tie, belt with metal gun studs, tan vest, black boots, felt hat. Circa 1967, #732.

143. Davy Crockett
8". Five-piece walker body, red fleece wig, tan suedene outfit of fringed jacket and pants, matching belt and boots, plush cap, metal rifle. Circa 1955, also came with black belt.

144. Davy Crockett Girl
8". Five-piece walker body, red wig, matching fringed outfit with skirt attached to olive top, boots, plush cap. Circa 1955.

145. American Indian Boy
8". Seven-piece tanned body, brunette wig, tagged "Indian Boy" outfit of tan vest, brown suedene pants with colored loincloth, headband, beads, bow, and tan slippers with brads. Circa 1966, #720.

146. American Indian Girl
8". Seven-piece tanned body, brunette braided wig, tagged "Madame Alexander" outfit of brown fringed suedene with trim, headband, beads, panty, tan slippers with brads, carries a papoose on her back. Circa 1966, #721.

147. Amish Boy
8". Seven-piece body, brunette short wig, tagged "Amish Boy" outfit of felt jacket (with hook and eye closure), black pants with attached white shirt, black hat, black socks and tie shoes. Circa 1966, #726, with original wrist tag.

148. Amish Girl
8". Seven-piece body, blonde wig pulled into back bun, tagged "Amish" outfit of grey full dress with black pinafore, black bonnet, long slip and pantaloon, black socks and boots. Circa 1966, #727, holds the Holy Bible.

149. Priscilla
8". Seven-piece body, blonde wig pulled atop head to the back, tagged dress with full white collar, apron, cap, slip, bloomers, white hose, black slippers, carries basket of fruit. Circa 1965-70, #729, with original wrist tag.

150. Colonial Girl
8". Seven-piece walker body, blonde wig pulled back over top of head, tagged polished cotton dress as described previously, same undergarments, basket of fruit. Circa 1962-64, #789, with original box.

151. Colonial Girl
8". Seven-piece walker body, blonde wig as before, tagged dress and undergarments as described previously. Circa 1962-64, #389, with plain cotton dress similar to the Priscilla outfit, showing how many variations there are.

152. Snow White
18". Five-piece body with Margaret face, black styled wig with pink satin ribbon, tagged gown of gold print on cream with attached cotton slip, gold lame vest, panty, socks and gold snap shoes. Circa 1952, #1835, with beauty box and fashion award tag.

153. Peter Pan
14". Five-piece body with Maggie face, tagged outfit of green felt top, tan tights, brown felt shoes, black belt, green cap with feather. Circa 1953, #1505, produced for one year only.

154. Cinderella
14". Five-piece body with Margaret face, blonde floss wig, tagged cotton dress with attached apron and patch, panty, kerchief, brown tie shoes. Circa 1950, with original broom.

154A. Alice in Wonderland
18". Five-piece body with Maggie face, blonde styled wig, tagged blue taffeta dress with organdy and lace pinafore, eyelet slip with matching tap pants (blue bows), hose, black shoes. Circa 1951, #1874, with original box.

155. Fashions of a Century Lady
18". Five-piece body with Margaret face, painted nails, blonde floss wig in braided and curled coiffure with flowers. Tagged apricot-colored taffeta gown with black velvet bodice and black lace accents, floral nosegay at waist, full slip with matching panty, net hose, gold pendant necklace, gold snap slippers. Circa 1954. From the Fashions of a Century series which featured elaborate gowns.

156. Lissy McGuffey Ana
12". Five-piece body, blonde braided wig, tagged red velvet jacket with plush collar, velvet skirt with attached taffeta top and plush mittens, tights, black shoes with red spats, plush hat with red pompom. Circa 1963, #1258, "Dolls from the Classics" series with original box and wrist tag, vivid coloring.

157. Wendy McGuffey Ana
8". Seven-piece body, blonde braided wig, tagged red gingham dress with eyelet pinafore, slip and pantaloon, cotton hose, white straw hat with flowers, black shoes. Circa 1965, #788.

158. Southern Belle
8". Seven-piece walker body, blonde wig, tagged "Madame Alexander" taffeta dress with lace rows, matching bonnet with fabric plume, slip and pantaloon, cotton hose, black slippers. Circa 1963, #385, with original wrist tag.

159. Lissy Southern Belle
12". Five-piece body, blonde wig styled in corkscrew curls, tagged blue taffeta dress with lace and satin ribbon accents, full slip and pantaloon, white socks, straw hat with pink and blue plumes, black shoes. Circa 1963, #1255, with original box and wrist tag. From the Lissy Classics series.

160. Southern Belle
8". Seven-piece walker body, blonde wig, tagged "Southern Belle" blue taffeta gown with undergarments as described previously. Circa 1963, #385, with hat flowers and lace rows variations.

The following are some of the lovely miniature portraits or "portrettes" as they were named. All use the Cissette adult-shaped, seven-piece body, assorted wig colors with special styles, blue eyeshadow and painted nails. The gowns are extremely detailed for their smaller size.

161. Godey
Tagged yellow taffeta gown with lace overlay, large taffeta ruffles at bottom, satin bow and lace accents, stiff petticoat, panty, yellow straw hat with tulle and flowers, gold shoes. Circa 1969, #1172.

162. Jenny Lind
Tagged pink satin gown with lace accents, flowers in hair and neckline, stiff petticoat, pantaloons, pink shoes. Circa 1969, #1171, with bouquet.

163. Southern Belle
Tagged white organdy gown with lace rows, red satin sash, stiff petticoat, pantaloons, white straw hat with tulle and flowers, white shoes. Circa 1970, #1185.

164. Godey
Tagged pink taffeta gown with lace overlay, ruffles and lace, stiff petticoat, pantaloons, straw hat, pink shoes. Circa 1969, #1172, with wrist tag.

165. Renoir
Tagged blue striped satin gown, velvet jacket, stiff slip, pantaloons, net hat with flowers, blue shoes. Circa 1970, #1180, with wrist tag.

166. Melanie
Tagged pink gown with net bodice, rows upon rows of lace, satin waist sash with flower, stiff petticoat, panty, hose, pink shoes. Circa 1969, #1173.

167. Melanie
Tagged yellow organdy gown with row upon row of lace, satin sash, floral accents, gold shoes. Circa 1970, #1182, original wrist tag.

168. Groom
8". Seven-piece walker body, reddish-brown wig, black suedene tailcoat over cream shirt attached to striped trouser, grey cummerbund and satin cravat with brilliant black socks and shoes. Circa 1956, #577.

169. Wendy Bride
8". Seven-piece walker body, blonde wig, tagged pleated tulle gown over attached slip, panty, veil with flowers, cream tie slippers. Circa 1956, #615, with original bouquet.

170. Wendy Bride
8". Seven-piece body, brunette wig, tagged tulle gown with lace borders and accents, puffed sleeves, attached slip, panty, matching veil with flowers, garter, cream slippers with rhinestones. Circa 1966, #735, with bouquet.

171. Wendy Bride
8". Seven-piece body, blonde wig, tagged pleated tulle gown with clover-style lace and faux pearl accents, attached slip, panty, veil with floral garland, cream tie slippers. Circa 1961, #480, with bouquet.

172. Wendy Bride
8". Seven-piece walker body, reddish-blonde wig, tagged "Wendy-Kin" gown of organdy with rows upon rows of lace, satin "V" sash, attached stiff petticoat, panty, veil with flowers, cream slippers with rhinestones. Circa 1964, #670, with original bouquet and wrist booklet.

173. Groom
18". Five-piece body with Margaret head, brunette mohair wig, black tailcoat with boutonniere, tagged white pique shirt front with attached cummerbund and pants, bow tie, rhinestone tac, watch chain, black socks and bow shoes. Circa 1949-50, #18.

174. Margaret Bride
18". Five-piece body, blonde mohair wig with barrettes and flowers, tagged silky tulle gown with satin bodice and peplum, lace accents, attached slip, panty, net hose, blue ribbon garter, cream bow shoes, matching veil. Circa 1949-50, with floral bouquet.

175. John Robert Powers Model
15". Five-piece body with Maggie face, blue eyes, blonde styled wig, tagged rose jersey bodysuit, grey flannel skirt with charms and chain, slip, hose, velvet beret, shoes. Circa 1952, with original personalized oval beauty box.

176. John Robert Powers Model
15". Five-piece body with Maggie face, brown eyes, blonde styled wig, tagged organdy blouse attached to panty, rhinestones on front and cuffs, bow tie, purple skirt with charms and chain, slip, hose, red beret, black shoes. Circa 1952, with original personalized oval beauty box.

177. McGuffey Ana in Larger Size
21". Five-piece body with Margaret face, blue eyes, strawberry-blonde mohair wig in braids with satin ribbon. Pink windowpane-check organdy dress with short puff sleeves and lace accents, eyelet slip with matching panty with pink bows, rayon hose, black shoes. Covered overall by purple velvet coat with picture collar and cuffs edged in fur, matching muff, purple felt bonnet with pale blue interior and flowers. Circa 1948-51. Popular McGuffey Ana character in stunning size with unusual color combination.

178. Cissette Travel Trousseau
10" doll. Case measures 10" W. x 12" H. Contains seven-piece adult body doll, blonde wig in tagged blue taffeta dress with polka dot sleeves and back panel, blue heels. Extra clothing includes pink nightgown with panty, yellow striped sun outfit and skirt, hat and shoes. Circa 1957, an FAO Schwarz exclusive.

179. Cissette Television at Home
10". Seven-piece adult body, auburn wig, lacy blouse with rhinestone buttons, black velvet pants, pink taffeta hip sash, pearl earrings, black heels. Circa 1957, #905, in original box.

180. Cissette Basic
10". Seven-piece adult body, blonde wig with bow, lace chemise, hose, flowery heels. Circa 1957, #900.

181. Cissette Television at Home
10". Seven-piece adult body, blonde wig, outfit as described for #179 but with yellow sash. Circa 1957, #905.

182. Cissette Basic with Box
10". Seven-piece adult body, auburn wig, tagged lace chemise, pearl earrings, hose, gold heels. Circa 1960, #700, with original box and booklets.

183. Cissy
20". Five-piece hard plastic body, vinyl bendable arms, blonde styled wig. Tagged yellow floral print taffeta day dress with black sash, lacy slip, panty, hose, pearl earrings, cameo, black hat with flowers, black heels. Circa 1957, #2120, with original price tag on skirt ($15.95).

184. Cissy
20". Five-piece hard plastic body, bendable vinyl arms, red wig, tagged green floral-print dress, pink satin sash with flowers, green slip with panty, green hat with flowers, hose, pearl earrings, green solitaire, black heels. Circa 1958, #2142.

185. Baby Angel
7 1/2". Five-piece body, blonde wig, tagged tulle gown with satin bodice and attached wings with clear beaded halo, organdy liner, panty, pearl necklace, cream tie slippers. Circa 1953, #480, with vivid coloring.

186. Wendy Ann Ballerina
7 1/2". Five-piece body, auburn wig, tagged pink tulle tutu with satin bodice, rhinestones, panty, floral coronet, pink tie slippers. Circa 1953.

187. Wendy Loves Ballet Lessons
8". Seven-piece walker body, blonde wig, bright pink tutu with flowers, floral circlet, pink tie slippers. Circa 1956, #564.

188. Wendy Loves Her Ballet Lessons
8". Seven-piece walker body, auburn wig, tagged white tutu with satin bodice, flower applique, matching panty, plastic roses on lace crown, pink tie slippers. Circa 1955, #454.

189. Wendy Ballerina
8". Seven-piece walker body, auburn wig, tagged pink tutu with satin bodice, rhinestone accents, panty, floral headpiece, pink tie slippers. Circa 1956.

190. Wendy Ann Walker
8". Five-piece walker body, blonde wig, tagged organdy dress with lace collar and flower accents, open net bonnet, slip, panty, red shoes. Circa 1955, #0615 boxed outfit.

191. Wendy Ann
7 1/2". Five-piece body, brunette wig, tagged organdy dress and undergarments as above, black shoes. Circa 1954.

192. Wendy Walker
8". Five-piece walker body, light-brown wig, tagged pink gingham dress with lace and ribbon accents, matching bonnet with flower, black shoes. Circa 1955.

193. Wendy Walker
8". Seven-piece walker body, brunette wig, pink cotton dress with light-blue pinafore, panty, pink straw hat with flowers, black shoes. Circa 1957.

194. Wendy Goes Shopping
8". Seven-piece walker body, tagged aqua polka dot dress with white collar and sleeves, slip, panty, white straw hat with flowers, purse, black shoes. Circa 1956, #593.

195. Picnic Day Lady
18". Five-piece walker body with Margaret face, auburn wig, tagged pink floral print gown with black lace edging, green and black fabric trim, green sash with formed back bows, cotton hoop skirt and panty, hose, straw picture hat with flowers and net, cream slippers. Circa 1953, #2001C, part of the Glamour Girl series with hat box.

196. Victorian Fashion Lady
18". Five-piece walker body with Maggie face, auburn wig, tagged pink taffeta gown with black velvet bodice and bands of black on the puff sleeves, waist garland of flowers and ribbons, slip with attached panty, hose, black net and lace bonnet with tulle bow. Circa 1953, #2010C, part of the Glamour Girls series with hat box.

197. Civil War Fashion Lady
18". Five-piece walker body with Margaret face, brunette wig, tagged cream taffeta gown with pink sash formed into wide back bows, roses accent the front gown, hoop slip with attached panty, hose, horsehair braid picture hat with flowers, cream slippers. Circa 1953, #2010B, Glamour Girls series with hat box.

198. Rosamund Bridesmaid
14". Five-piece walker body with Maggie face, dark blonde wig, tagged pink tulle gown with floral accents, panty, hose, bandeau with flowers, cream slippers. Circa 1953, #1551, with hat box.

199. Peggy Bride
14". Five-piece body, blonde mohair wig, pink organdy gown with peter pan collar, waist sash, attached liner, panty, hose, blue ribbon garter, veil attached to bandeau with flowers, cream slippers. Circa 1950, this gown came in white and pastel colors.

200. Rosamund Bridesmaid
14". Five-piece walker body with Maggie face, blonde wig, tagged pink tulle gown with floral accents, panty, hose, bandeau with flowers, cream slippers. Circa 1953, #1551, with hat box.

201. Wendy Bride
14". Seven-piece body, blonde wig, tagged "Wendy Bride" gown of oyster-white taffeta with floral accents, hoop slip, panty, hose, bandeau with flowers and veil, cream slippers. Circa 1955, #1551, holding bouquet.

202. Wendy Bride with Box
18". Five-piece walker body, blonde wig, tagged in nylon tulle-over-taffeta gown, panty, hose, garter, veil is attached to a starched lace bonnet with flowers, cream slippers. Circa 1954, #1855, in original box.

203. Prince Phillip/Groom
18". Five-piece walker body with Margaret face, red caracul wig, tagged pique tuxedo shirt with bow tie, rhinestone tac, attached cummerbund and pants, tailcoat, watch chain, black socks and shoes. Circa 1953, also was used as Prince Phillip for the Queen Elizabeth portrait of the same year.

204. Little Genius with Box
8". Tagged pink organdy dress with ribbon and lace, matching bonnet, slip, flannel diaper, bottle. Circa 1956, in box marked #755.

205. Little Genius
8". Two-piece pink stripe playsuit, lacy bonnet with bows, booties. Circa 1957, #105.

206. Littlest Kitten
8". Five-piece vinyl baby body, white-blonde rooted wig, tagged organdy coatdress, slip, flannel diaper, booties. Circa 1963, #550.

207. Little Genius
8". Long Christening gown with large collar, matching slip and bonnet, flannel diaper, booties. Circa 1960.

208. Little Genius
8". Tagged long Christening gown with matching slip and bonnet, organdy diaper, booties. Circa 1957.

209. Little Genius with Box
8". Tagged pink striped cotton romper, eyelet bonnet and booties in box marked #100. Circa 1958.

Note - All Little Genius' have a vinyl five-piece baby body with hard plastic heads with open mouths for drinking and blonde plush wigs.

210. Farmer
10". One-piece latex body, vinyl head marked Alexander with molded and painted features. Tagged green and purple plaid

shirt, yellow overalls with matching sunhat, plastic tools, socks, cream shoes. Circa 1951, #620B, with original yellow box.

211. Maggie Mixup
8". Seven-piece walker body, red wig, green eyes, freckles, smile, tagged red top with hearts, striped pants with felt flowers, gold sandals. Circa 1961, with original wooden toy.

212. Maggie Mixup
8". Seven-piece walker body and head as described above, pink cotton dress sold as boxed outfit with tagged panty with pink bows, black shoes. Circa 1960.

213. Maggie Skater
8". Seven-piece walker body and head as described in #211, knit unitard, pink felt skirt with tulle and felt flowers, matching hat, tie skates. Circa 1961, #626.

214. Little Lady
8". Seven-piece walker body with Maggie face, brunette wig pulled back atop head into ponytail, tagged "Little Lady Doll" aqua dress with chintz polka dot pinafore, full petticoat, pantaloons, black shoes and gaiters. Circa 1960, from the packaged gift box set.

215. Set of Little Women Characters
8". Set of five Little Women with seven-piece walker bodies and Laurie with a seven-piece body. All have tagged outfits as shown from the 1960 series, Laurie is from 1966.

216. Little Women Amy with Box
8". Seven-piece body, blonde styled wig, tagged white chintz dress with yellow dotted pinafore, petticoat, pantaloons, black shoes. Circa 1962, #7811, with wrist booklet.

217. Little Women Jo with Box
8". Seven-piece walker body, brunette styled wig with ribbon, tagged red chintz dress with organdy neck piece and sleeves, star design on dress, petticoat, pantaloons, black shoes. Circa 1959, #781.

218. Little Women Beth with Box
8". Seven-piece body, brunette styled wig with ribbon, tagged pink dress with organdy pinafore, petticoat, pantaloons, black shoes. Circa 1962, #781.

219. Set of Four Little Women

14". Four five-piece bodies with Margaret and Maggie faces, styled wigs, tagged outfits of taffeta, cottons and laces with slips, pantaloons and black bow shoes. Circa 1951, includes Marme, Beth, Meg and Amy with rarer braids.

220. American Girl with Box
8". Seven-piece walker body, blonde braided wig, tagged red gingham dress with eyelet pinafore, petticoat, bloomers, knit hose, straw hat with flowers and ribbon, black shoes. Circa 1962, #388, in original box with gold wrist tag.

221. American Girl
8". As described in previous lot but with dress material and hat flower variations. Circa 1963-64, with wrist booklet.

222. Wendy Ann
7 1/2". Five-piece body, blonde wig pulled into pigtails, tagged yellow dress with matching panty, flowered pinafore, straw hat, black shoes. Circa 1953, with unusual hairstyle.

223. Wendy Quiz-kin
7 1/2". Five-piece Quiz-kin body, auburn wig, tagged organdy top attached to panty matching print of the jumper, lacy bonnet, black shoes. Circa 1953, with original price tag and wrist tag.

224. Wendy Walker
8". Five-piece walker body, blonde wig, tagged yellow dress, grey striped pinafore, slip, panty, straw hat with flowers, black shoes. Circa 1954.

225. Scarlett
8". Seven-piece body, brunette wig, green eyes, tagged "Scarlett O'Hara", green floral print long dress with satin sash, lace accents, hem ruffle, slip and pantaloon, picture hat, black shoes. Circa 1966, #725.

226. Scarlett
8". Seven-piece body, brunette wig, brown eyes, tagged "Scarlett", pink floral long dress with satin sash, lace accents, hem ruffle, slip, pantaloons, picture hat, black shoes. Circa mid-late 1960's. Rare fabric and color version of dress for this doll.

227. Scarlett
8". Seven-piece body, brunette wig, green eyes, tagged "Scarlett", pink and green floral long dress with satin sash, hem ruffle, slip, pantaloons, picture hat, black shoes. Circa 1970.

228. Southern Belle
7 1/2". Five-piece body, blonde wig, organdy gown with lace accents, tulle sleeves, matching bonnet with flowers, pink slip and pantaloons, blue shoes. Circa 1954, with original wrist tag.

228A. Melanie
8". Seven-piece walker body, brunette wig pulled in back, green velvet gown with red "jewel" on bodice, full petticoat, pantaloons, pearl necklace, black shoes. Circa 1956,

229. Cissy Queen Elizabeth
20". Five-piece body with two-piece vinyl arms, blonde styled wig, tagged "Cissy" cream brocade gown with blue Sash of the Garter with Star, mitts, full taffeta petticoat, panty, hose, bracelets, earrings, necklace, jeweled crown and silver heels. Circa 1956, #2042.

230. Queen Elizabeth
8". Five-piece walker body, blonde wig, tagged gown of cream brocade satin, blue ribbon sash, slip and panty, red velvet robe with gold trim, jeweled crown, gold slippers. Circa 1955, #499, with gown fabric variation.

231. Wendy Bride with Box
18". Five-piece walker body, blonde wig, tagged gown of tulle covered taffeta, panty, hose, garter, veil with attached bandeau and flowers, bouquet, cream slippers. Circa 1953, #1852, with original box.

232. Wendy Bride with Box
18". Five-piece walker body with two-piece vinyl arms, red wig, oyster-white taffeta gown with braid, flower and rhinestone accents, veil attached to net bandeau, slip, panty, hose, garter, tulle muff with flowers, pearl necklace, cream slippers. Circa 1955, #1851, in original box.

233. Wendy At Sunday Breakfast
8". Five-piece walker body, brunette wig, tagged taffeta dress with lace and floral ribbon trim, matching panty, black shoes. Circa 1956, #536.

234. Wendy Walker
8". Seven-piece walker body, dark blonde wig, tagged pink taffeta dress with lace and flowers, slip, panty, pink straw hat with flowers, white shoes. Circa 1956.

235. Wendy Time for School
8". Seven-piece walker body, auburn wig, tagged cotton dress with white collar, open lace accents, slip, panty, straw hat, blue shoes. Circa 1957, #359.

236. Wendy Nurse
8". Seven-piece walker body, auburn wig, tagged outfit of blue striped dress with white pinafore, cap, panty, tie shoes, holds small plastic baby. Circa 1962, #363, in box marked 460 but with price and "Nurse" in pencil.

237. Wendy Nurse
8". Seven-piece walker body, auburn wig, tagged outfit as described above. Circa 1962, #363, with baby outfit variation.

238. Groom
8". Five-piece walker body, red plush wig, tagged suedene shirt with attached striped pants, tan cummerbund, grey silk cravat and rhinestone tac, black suedene tailcoat, black socks and shoes. Circa 1956, #577, with box marked #300 Brown.

239. Wendy Bride
8". Seven-piece walker body, blonde wig, tagged tulle gown with satin sash, slip, panty, circlet of flowers with attached veil, bouquet, cream slippers. Circa 1959, #483.

240. Wendy Bridesmaid
8". Five-piece walker body, blonde wig, tagged pink tulle gown with organdy liner, panty, headband of flowers and leaves, bouquet, cream tie slippers. Circa 1955, #478, in box marked #451.

241. Wooden Doll Trunk with Outfits
20" W. x 9" H. x 10" D. Light pine lift-lid trunk with pull-out tray by Pearline of Michigan. Includes assorted loose Alexander clothing and hats from mixed years, boxed outfits #313, #340 and four pairs of packaged socks and shoes.

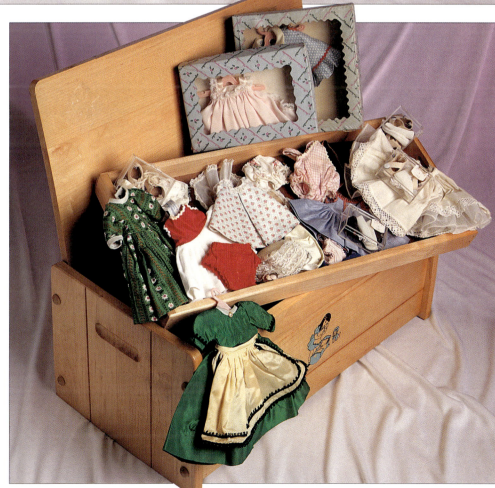

242. Elise Golden Ballerina
17". Seven-piece adult body with bendable vinyl arms, blonde styled wig, tagged "Elise" tutu of golden net, cloth and sequins, pink tights, sequined tiara, earrings, golden ballet shoes. Circa 1959, #1810, made for one year only.

243. Cissette Golden Ballerina
10". Seven-piece adult body, blonde wig, tagged "Cissette" tutu and tiara as described previously. Circa 1959, #713, made for one year only.

244. Pair of Boxed Little Genius Outfits
Style numbers 0123-polka dot robe and 0209-pink robe.

245. Pair of Boxed Wendy-Kin Dresses
Style numbers 0326-pink taffeta and lace and 0312-red polka dot dress.

246. Boxed Wendy Riding Habit
Style #0355 from 1962.

247. Pair of Boxed Wendy Outfits
Style numbers 0310-turquoise coat and bonnet and 0451-pink and blue skating outfit.

248. Cynthia
18". Five-piece brown body, black styled wig, brown eyes, tagged pink organdy dress with lace and ruffles, satin sash, attached slip, panty, black shoes. Circa 1952, #1830, with original beauty box and fashion award tag. A hard-to-find model with vivid, fresh coloring.

COMB and CURLERS FOR YOUR Madam Alexander DOLL

249. Mary Martin
18". Five-piece body, red caracul wig, brown eyes, tagged cotton sailor outfit with cap, white socks, black shoes. Circa 1950. Outfit from the movie "South Pacific" as stated on the clothing tag.

250. Story Princess
15". Five-piece walker body, brunette wig, tagged aqua taffeta gown with flowers, panty, hose, sequin tiara, silver slippers. Circa 1954, #1560, with bottom of original box.

251. Lissy Cinderella
12". Five-piece body, blonde styled wig, tagged "Cinderella" gown of blue satin, lace, flowers and sequins, slip and panty, hose, jeweled tiara, silver slippers. Circa 1966, #1235. Also came as Poor Cinderella and in a gift box with both outfits.

252. Golden Infant of Prague
8". Seven-piece walker body with molded upright arms, hands and fingers; reddish-brown sheepskin wig, robe and cape of woven golden fabric with rose satin lining, full-length slip, jewelled cross, panty, golden crown of same material lining and iridescent "jewels", magenta sandals. Circa 1957, with extra slip.

253. Royal Purple Infant of Prague
8". Seven-piece walker body as previously described, reddish-brown sheepskin wig, robe and cape of royal purple jacquard with gold trim, full-length slip, panty, golden 14K cross, golden crown of same material lining and blue "jewels", cream slippers and world globe. Circa 1957.

Both of these dolls came from the original West Coast owner who said they were a gift from nuns at a local parish. The dolls were ordered from Alexander who also supplied the outer crowns and shoes. It is not known if the dolls had the arms molded prior to leaving the factory but they were special ordered by a religious supply company and dressed by an order of nuns in the Midwest.

254. Greek Boy with Box
8". Seven-piece body, brunette short wig, brown eyes, dressed as shown. Circa 1965-68, #769, with original box and wrist booklet.

255. Greek Girl
8". Seven-piece body, brunette wig, tagged "Greece" outfit as shown. Circa 1968-72, #765.

256. Turkey
8". Seven-piece body, brunette wig, dressed as shown. Circa 1968-72, #787, with original box and wrist booklet.

257. India
8". Seven-piece body, brunette wig pulled into back braid, tagged outfit as shown with golden sandals and assorted jewelry. Circa 1965-70, #775, with paler complexion.

258. India
8". Seven-piece tanned body as described above with similar outfit, tan sandals. Circa 1970-72, #775, with original box and wrist booklet.

259. African
8". Seven-piece brown body, black fleecy wig, brown eyes, tagged outfit as shown. Circa 1966-71, #766, with wrist booklet.

260. Morocco
8". Seven-piece tanned body, brunette wig, black eyes, tagged outfit as shown, golden slippers. Circa 1968-70, #762, with original box.

261. Eskimo
8". Seven-piece brown body, short brunette wig, brown eyes, tagged outfit as shown. Circa 1967-69, #723, with wrist booklet.

262. Miss USA
8". Seven-piece body, blonde wig, tagged gown as shown, golden slippers and tiara. Circa 1966-68, #728, from the Americana series with original box and tag.

263. Hawaii
8". Seven-piece brown body, brunette wig, outfit as shown. Circa 1966-69, #722, with wrist tag.

264. Scots Lass
8". Seven-piece walker body, brunette wig, tagged outfit as shown with slip and panty. Circa 1964-72, #796.

265. Irish
8". Seven-piece body, red wig, tagged outfit as shown with full slip and pantaloon. Circa 1964, #778, in original box with wrist booklet and $7.50 price tag.

266. English Guard
8". Seven-piece body, short brunette wig, tagged outfit as shown. Circa 1967-68, #764, with wrist tag.

267. One-of-a-kind "Christine" Portrait Doll from Phantom of the Opera 21". Seven-piece adult body with vinyl arms, frosted blonde elaborately curled and hand-styled wig, Jacqueline portrait face with coral painted lips, blue eyes with hand-painted eyelashes and feathered brows, smoky eyeshadow. She wears a tagged, hand-made draped gown of ciel blue silk with boned bodice, embellished with lace, pearls and sequins with taffeta pleating at the hem and tiny buttons down the back with a tulle and chiffon bustle train. Undergarments include a stiff petticoat, pantaloons, boned bustle, hose and matching heels. Lace mitts, a brilliant ring and "crystal" earrings and necklace complete the ensemble. Circa 1990. Comes with additional lace and tulle bridal veil, bouquet with formed ceramic and silk flowers, phantom mask, and certificate of authenticity.

Based on an idea by Bill Birnbaum, this was the first doll after the change of directors at the Alexander Company that was produced by new designers exclusively for the 1990 Walt Disney World Auction. Christine's bridal gown is styled after the fashions of the 1880's and was created and hand-made by designers Daun Fallon and Annette Shelley. A letter accompanies the doll from Ms. Fallon and gives an insight as to the ideas behind the costuming and its construction.

268. One-of-a-kind Doll "It's A Girl"
21". Seven-piece adult body with vinyl arms, dark blonde human hair wig in Gibson Girl style, Cissy portrait face with blue eyes, hand-painted eyelashes and feathered brows, rose-colored lips. She wears typical Victorian underwear of boned corset, boned bustle back, silk chemise and bloomers, hose and garters. Two dresses are included - a day dress and evening gown, both with layers of organdy, lace, ribbon, silk and hand embroidery. A flowery picture hat, lace-up satin boots, gusseted hand-painted kid gloves, handkerchief, and silver metal purse complete the ensembles. She is accompanied by a white metal and wicker pram decorated with flowers, holding the cherished new baby girl in a complimentary organdy gown and bonnet. Circa 1992. Comes with Certificate of Authenticity.

This stunning labor of love was created by Alexander designers Daun Fallon and Therese Stadelmeier for the 1992 Walt Disney World Auction. 1993 was the re-introduction year for the Little Genius baby and the artist's proof (the first doll produced) is the baby that is presented here. The dolls appeared on the cover of the 1993 Alexander catalogue and in a feature article by a national doll magazine which is included. This is probably the most detailed doll ever produced by the company.

269. One-of-a-kind Doll "Queen Isabella of Spain"
21". Seven-piece adult body with vinyl arms, reddish-brown curled and braided wig, Jacqueline portrait face with hand-painted eyelashes, feathered brows and brushed coral lips. Gown of panne velvet with jeweled accents, gold braid, lace and lame trim, braided tapestry cloak, golden mesh wimple, jeweled veil and elaborate crown, gold beaded necklace and "emerald" rectangular solitaire, she holds a "parchment" map. Undergarments include a tulle, net and lace slip, pantaloons, hose and black kid heels. Circa 1991. Created for the 1991 Walt Disney World Auction by designer Daun Fallon, this was the cover doll for the 1992 Madame Alexander Company catalogue.

270. One-of-a-kind "The Emperor and the Nightingale"
The Emperor is a 26" fully-jointed, plush black bear with leather paws, French yarn nose and glass eyes. His court robe is designed of iridescent silk, multi-colored brocade and gold embroidery, with a chinese red silk undergarment, glass bead necklaces, the hat and shoes are of velvets with beading, gold trims and various gold braidwork and accents. The 8" Nightingale wears a hand-painted iridescent bodysuit and is covered with individual green and blue feathers and has a burgundy velvet cushion on which to stand. Circa 1992. Also included is the Certificate of Authenticity and a copy of the story, originally written by Hans Christian Anderson.

Created for the 1992 Walt Disney World Auction. Alexander designers Daun Fallon and Therese Stadelmeier created the clothing and Rita Raiffe designed the one-of-a-kind bear for Gund. This pairing of doll and teddy bear marked the joint venture of Madame Alexander and Gund and was to be the premiere project in a collaboration between the two companies for a series of bears. However, it was an ill-fated partnership and never reached the production stages for the line thus making the above the only items ever produced under the pairing of the two companies. The Bear and Doll appeared on the cover of a 1992 issue of "Teddy Bear and Friends" magazine.

271. Wendy Attends a House Party
8". Seven-piece walker body, braided auburn wig, tagged dress of polished cotton with taffeta pinafore, slip, panty, straw hat, flowers, basket, and brown shoes. Circa 1956, #582.

272. Wendy with Flower Basket
8". Seven-piece walker body, blonde wig pulled into pigtails with flowers, cotton dress with eyelet pinafore, panty, black shoes, and flower basket. Circa 1957.

273. Wendy Rides Well
8". Seven-piece walker body, blonde wig, tagged shirt, brown jodhpurs, riding hat, crop, and boots. Circa 1956, #571.

274. Wendy Riding Habit with Box
8". Seven-piece body, brunette braided wig, tagged knit top, brown houndstooth jodhpurs, riding hat, crop, boots. Circa 1965, #623, with original box.

275. Wendy Riding Habit
8". Seven-piece walker body, blonde braided wig, outfit as described in 274. Circa 1965, #623.

276. Wendy Dude Ranch
8". Five-piece walker body, blonde wig, yellow shirt, jeans with red trim, sombrero, and boots. Circa 1955, #449.

277. Early Wendy-Kin
7 1/2". Five-piece body, brunette wig, tagged cotton sundress with blue gingham border, matching hat, panty, blue shoes. Circa 1953.

278. Early Wendy-Kin
7 1/2". Five-piece body, blonde wig, tagged pink taffeta jumper- over-organdy blouse attached to taffeta panty, matching bonnet, black shoes. Circa 1953.

279. Wendy Going Calling
8". Seven-piece walker body, blonde wig, tagged taffeta dress with lace, buttons and sash, slip, panty, straw hat with flowers, black shoes. Circa 1957, #387.

280. Wendy-Kin
8". Five-piece walker body, blonde wig, tagged pink cotton dress with rickrack trim, slip, panty, pink straw hat with flowers and turned-up back, cream shoes. Circa 1956, doll in later #529 School Days dress.

281. Wendy-Kin Day Dress
8". Seven-piece walker body, auburn wig, tagged chambray dress with organdy pinafore, panty, pink straw hat with flowers, black shoes. Circa 1956.

282. Cissy Bride
20". Seven-piece adult body with vinyl bendable arms, styled blonde wig, tagged tulle and satin gown with brocade accents, stiff slip, veil attached to floral coronet, pearl necklace, solitaire engagement ring, brilliant earrings, silver heels. Circa 1955, #2101.

283. Cissy's Dancing Dress
20". Seven-piece adult body with vinyl bendable arms, styled blonde wig with flowers, tagged pink pleated tulle and lace dress with floral accents and pearl neckline, satin sash with flower drape, panty, hose, solitaire ring, silver heels. Circa 1956, #2025, with original box and hat box.

284. Cissy's Gown of Great Beauty
20". Seven-piece adult body with vinyl bendable arms, styled blonde wig, tagged tulle gown painted with flowers, rhinestone and floral accents, a big picture hat, mitts, pearl earrings and bracelet, solitaire ring, panty, hose, and glittery heels. Circa 1958, #2282.

285. Cissy Bridesmaid
20". Seven-piece adult body with vinyl bendable arms, styled blonde wig, gown of blue pleated tulle and silvery net bodice with pearl neckline, rhinestone accents, satin sash, tulle headpiece with flowers, panty, hose, blue heels. Circa 1956, #2030.

286. Binnie Walker Formal
17". Seven-piece flat-footed body with vinyl bendable arms, styled blonde wig, tagged tulle pleated gown with net bodice, satin sash, panty, hose, bandeau with rosebuds, silver slippers. Circa 1956, similar to the Wendy Bride of the same year.

287. Cissy Accessories in Box and Rack.
A dazzling group of accessories and jewelry for Cissy in original box. Circa 1957, #22-91, with turquoise wooden clothing rack (not illustrated).

287A. Cissy Clothing Racks (Not Illustrated)
Pair of pink wooden clothing racks for Cissy or larger dolls with original brown wrapping and label with style #67.

288. Cissette Ballerina
10". Blonde styled wig with flowers, tagged pink tulle tutu with flowers, satin suit, pink tights, rhinestone earrings, pink vinyl ballet slippers. Circa 1958, #823, with original box.

289. Cissette Ballerina
10". Brunette styled wig, white satin tutu, hose, pearl earrings, ink vinyl slippers. Circa 1957, #914.

290. Cissette Formal
10". Dark blonde styled wig, tagged gown of ruffles and organdy with satin sash and flower, stiff slip, lace chemise, hose and pink heels. Circa 1963, #745.

290A. Cissette Bride
10". Dark blonde wig, painted fingernails, tagged gown of tulle with satin bodice and sash, veil attached to coronet of flowers, panty, bouquet, brilliant earrings, gold heels. Circa 1957, the cover outfit on the introductory brochure.

291. Cissette Bride
10". Tosca wig, tagged gown of tulle with lacy bodice, satin sash, bouquet, veil attached to floral garland, panty, hose, pink heels. Circa 1957, #0980, sold as an extra outfit.

292. Cissette Bridesmaid
10". Auburn styled wig, gown of pink swiss-dotted tulle with floral accents, satin sash with bow back, pearl drop earrings, picture horsehair hat, panty, hose, gold heels. Circa 1957, #960.

Note - All Cissettes have a seven-piece adult hard plastic body.

293. Fashion Lady in Riding-Style Outfit
18". Five-piece body, Margaret face with hand-painted eyelashes and brows, red accent dots at eye corners, rose mouth, reddish-brown mohair wig. Tagged outfit of green taffeta riding-style jacket with lacy jabot insert and collar, velvet ties, matching long skirt, long slip with lace hem, rayon hose, black shoes with bows. Circa late 1940's. Unusual outfit not identified previously and hand-painted facial features similar to the later portrait series.

294. Lissy Bridesmaid with Box
12". Nine-piece body, black eyes, blonde styled wig, tagged pleated tulle gown with silver net bodice, panty, hose, tulle bandeau with flowers, bouquet, rhinestone bracelet, blue heels. Circa 1956, #1248, with wrist tag in original box.

295. Lissy Sunday School
12". Nine-piece body, blue eyes, brunette styled wig, bright blue organdy dress with val lace and feather stitching, slip, panty, straw hat with flowers, anklets and heels. Circa 1956, #1241, in original box.

296. Lissy Jo
12". Nine-piece body, brunette styled wig, tagged blue taffeta dress with red floral print pinafore, cotton slip and pantaloon, anklets, and black heels. Circa 1957, in later box marked #1322 and with original department store price tag.

297. Lissy Amy
12". Five-piece body, blonde styled wig, blue pique cotton dress with organdy pinafore, stiff petticoat, pantaloons, anklets, black shoes. Circa 1961, #1225, with original box.

298. Lissy Meg
12". Five-piece body, tosca styled wig, tagged purple stripe dress, cotton pinafore, stiff petticoat, pantaloons, anklets, black shoes. Circa 1962, #1225, with original box.

299. Lissy Meg
12". Nine-piece body, blonde styled wig, tagged blue dress with striped pinafore, cotton slip and pantaloons, anklets, black heels. Circa 1957, #1225, with original box and tag.

300. Lissy Jo
12". Five-piece body, brunette styled wig, tagged black and white polka dot dress with red pinafore, stiff petticoat, pantaloons, anklets, black shoes. Circa 1962, #1225, in original box.

301. Margot Ballerina
14". Seven-piece body, red styled wig with flowers, tagged blue tutu with flowers, pink tights, cream slippers. Circa 1955, #1541. Fresh and vivid coloring.

302. Margot Ballerina
18". Five-piece walker body, blonde styled wig with flowers, pink satin and tulle tutu with rhinestones, pink hose, cream slippers. Circa 1954, #1850.

303. Nina Ballerina
14". Five-piece body, styled blonde floss wig with flowers, tagged pink satin and organdy tutu with gold trim and floral accents, gold ribbon choker, pink slippers. Circa 1950.

304. Maggie Walker
14". Five-piece walker body, red styled wig, tagged "Maggie" plaid shirt, gabardine skirt, belt with rhinestones and brads, slip, panty, socks, black tie shoes. Circa 1952, #2016.

305. Kathy Skater
14". Five-piece body, braided brown floss wig, tagged knit bodysuit, pink skating skirt, pink felt cummerbund and matching felt bandeau with flowers, brown tie roller skates. Circa 1951, in original box with hard-to-find cummerbund.

306. Easter Presentation Egg
A floral-papered German egg holds an 8" seven-piece body Wendy-kins with blonde wig, tagged yellow sunsuit, white sandals and basket with bunny, a yellow chick rests on the other side of the egg filled with cello-grass. Circa 1966. Another version of this hard-to-find piece.

307. Easter Girl
8". Seven-piece body, brunette wig, tagged yellow polished cotton dress with lace bodice and flower, matching lacy bonnet, tights, tan shoes. Circa 1968, in box marked #719 with wrist tag. Limited edition of 300 made only for the West Coast.

99

308. Cissette Day Dress
Tosca wig, tagged pink gingham dress with rose print, rhinestone accents, pink slip and panty, pearl earrings, red heels. Circa 1957.

309. Cissette Day Dress
Blonde wig, tagged bright pink dress with lace edges, panty, hose, pearl earrings, gold heels. Circa 1957.

310. Cissette Cocktail Dress
Blonde wig, tagged navy taffeta dress with tulle cap sleeves, organdy collar tie, panty, hose, black heels. Circa 1957.

311. Madame Alexander Furniture
9" L. x 5" H. Turquoise tufted sateen divan with gold trim around bottom edges, metal legs. Circa 1956, #80, with original label on bottom.

All Cissettes have seven-piece hard plastic adult bodies.

312. Scarlett Portrette
Brunette styled wig, green eyes, tagged taffeta gown as shown with matching bonnet, full slip, pantyhose, black heels. Circa 1973, #1180, with original box and wrist tag.

313. Queen Portrette
Tosca styled wig with crown, tagged white brocade gown as pictured, full slip, panty, hose, white shoes. Circa 1972, #1186, in original box with tag.

314. Agatha Portrette
Brunette styled wig, tagged red velvet gown as pictured with matching hat, full slip, pantaloons, red velvet heels. Circa 1968, #1171.

315. Southern Belle Portrette
Brunette styled wig, tagged ruffled organdy gown as shown with picture hat, full slip, pantaloons, white heels. Circa 1973, #1184, with original box and tag.

All 10" Portrettes have seven-piece adult bodies with blue eyeshadow and painted nails.

316. Binnie Walker
18". Nine-piece body with bendable vinyl arms, blonde styled wig, tagged pink cotton dress, knit cardigan with rhinestone and floral accents, matching cap, hoop skirt, panty, anklets, and black shoes. Circa 1955, #1827. Wendy had a matching outfit this year.

317. Wendy Bedtime
8". Seven-piece walker body, blonde wig in pigtails, floral nylon nightie, panty, pink slippers. Circa 1960.

318. Wendy's Crepe Pajamas
8". Five-piece walker body, blonde wig, pink crepe pajamas with floral-print robe, pink pompom slippers. Circa 1956, #021 pajama, #012 robe, both boxed sets.

319. Wendy Walker
8". Seven-piece walker body, blonde wig, tagged red windowpane-check taffeta dress with matching panty, hat with berries, red shoes. Circa 1959.

320. Wendy Walker
8". Five-piece walker body, tosca wig, tagged blue polka dotted dress with matching panty, straw hat with flowers. Circa 1956.

321. Wendy Walker
8". Seven-piece walker body, blonde wig, tagged red and white striped dress, panty, white straw hat, black shoes. Circa 1957.

322. Wendy Day Dress
8". Seven-piece walker body, auburn wig, tagged green polished cotton dress with organdy pinafore, slip, panty, straw hat with flower, green shoes. Circa 1956.

323. Wendy Has Many School Frocks
8". Seven-piece walker body, blonde braided wig, tagged plaid dress with matching panty, tucked pinafore, straw hat with flowers, green shoes. Circa 1957, #368.

324. Wendy in Gabardine Coat
8". Seven-piece walker body, blonde wig, tagged blue coat with white collar and cuffs, red taffeta dress and panty underneath, straw hat, black shoes. Circa 1956.

325. Wendy in Velvet Coat
8". Five-piece walker body, blonde wig, green velvet coat, white fur hat and muff, white taffeta dress, slip and panty, white shoes. Circa 1956.

326. Wendy in Gabardine Coat
8". Five-piece walker body, brunette wig, tagged blue coat with white collar and cuffs, dress of white top attached to pleated blue skirt, panty, red straw hat with flowers, black shoes. Circa 1955.

The following Little Women dolls all have five-piece bodies and the outfits are as shown with all having a long slip, pantaloons, socks, and black bow shoes underneath.

327. Little Women Amy
14". Body with larger hands, Margaret face, blonde styled wig, tagged dress as shown. Circa 1955, #1500.

328. Little Women Meg
14". Margaret face, blonde styled wig, tagged dress as shown. Circa 1952, #1500, with original box, wrist tag, and beauty box with Fashion Academy Award.

328A. Little Women Beth
14". Body with larger hands, Maggie face, brunette styled wig, tagged outfit as shown. Circa 1955, #1500.

329. Little Women Jo
14". Maggie face, brunette styled wig, tagged green dress as shown. Circa 1952, #1500, in original box with Fashion Academy Award tag.

330. Little Women Marme
14". Body with larger hands, Margaret face, brunette styled wig, tagged outfit as shown. Circa 1955, #1500, with original beauty box.

330A. Little Women Beth
14". Maggie face, brunette styled wig, tagged outfit as shown. Circa 1952, #1500, with Fashion Academy tag and beauty box.

331. Marybel with Case
16". Six-piece swivel-waist body, vinyl head with rooted blonde hair, brown eyes, tagged satin romper with pompom slippers. Comes complete in case with assorted casts, crutches, glasses, band-aids to help her get well. Circa 1960, #1575.

332. Sweet Tears
14". Five-piece baby body, open mouth, rooted blonde hair, tagged pink cotton dress and panty in layette set as pictured. Circa 1968, #3678, with original sleeve.

333. Muffin
14". Cloth baby with yellow plush hair, felt features, tagged organdy dress and flannel diaper. Circa 1967, #75, in original box with tag.

334. Funny
18". Pink and white gingham cloth doll with yarn hair, material features, tagged patchwork jumper, bloomers, orange shoes. Circa 1974, #60, with original box and tags.

335. Sweet Tears
14". Five-piece baby body, open mouth, rooted brunette hair, tagged pink cotton dress with floral ribbon trim in layette set as pictured. Circa 1968, #3678.

336. Edith the Lonely Doll
16". Six-piece swivel-waist body with vinyl Kelly head, blue eyes, rooted blonde styled wig, tagged pink gingham dress with apron, slip, panty, anklets, black shoes. Circa 1959, #1650, with wrist tag and a copy of the Dare Wright book.

337. Pollyanna
16". Six-piece swivel-waist body with vinyl Kelly head, blue eyes, rooted blonde braided wig, tagged bright pink dress with black trim, slip, panty, cotton hose, straw hat, black bow tie shoes. Circa 1960, #1530, with original box and tag.

338. Snow White
14". Five-piece body, rooted brunette wig, black eyes, tagged gown of yellow with blue velvet bodice, scarlet and white robe, stiff slip, panty, hose, black slippers. Circa 1967-77, #1455, in original box with tag. A Disneyland exclusive.

339. Cinderella's Ball Gown
For a 14" doll. Tagged blue taffeta gown with velvet bodice and gold trim, petticoat and panty. Circa 1969, #140, with original box. An exclusive for FAO Schwarz.

DRESS		HAIR		
PINK	BLUE	MAISE	BLONDE	AUBURN
RED	GREEN	WHITE	TOSCA	BROWN
ACQUA	ROSE	LAV.	**EYES**	
NAVY	CHART.	BEAUTY	BLUE	BROWN

Madame *Alexander*

JACQUELINE 2210

ALEXANDER DOLL COMPANY, N.Y., N.Y.

340. Jacqueline Portrait
21". Seven-piece body having vinyl one-piece arms, blue eyeshadow, rooted brunette styled wig, painted nails. Tagged pink satin gown with pink lace cover-up with rhinestone, pearl and flower accents, mitts, twin pearl necklace, pearl and brilliant earrings in a sunburst setting, solitaire ring, stiff slip, panty, hose, silver heels. Circa 1961, the outfit is supposedly called "Embassy Tea" though it never appeared in an Alexander catalogue.

341. Jacqueline Portrait
21". Seven-piece body having vinyl one-piece arms, blue eyeshadow, rooted brunette styled wig, painted nails. Tagged white satin strapless gown with silver and white satin trim, matching full-length coat with opera collar, full slip, panty, hose, pearl beaded purse, pearl bracelet, solitaire ring, double pearl necklace, pearl and rhinestone sunburst earrings, silver heels. Circa 1961, #2210, in the original box.

This is the only doll that Madame Alexander ever forecast as becoming a collector's item.

342. Nancy Drew
12". Five-piece body, rooted red-dish blonde bouffant wig, tagged white coat with matching white sheath dress, green scarf, boots, purse, and camera. Circa 1967, #1262, with wrist tag.

343. Poor Cinderella
12". Five-piece body, rooted blonde wig, tagged dress of olive cotton with orange apron, head-scarf, panty, anklets, and brown slippers. Circa 1967, with original broom and wrist tag.

344. Elise Bride
18". Eleven-piece body having jointed ankles and bendable vinyl arms, blonde styled wig, tagged gown of tulle with ruffles at bodice and hem, veil attached to a coronet of flowers, stiff slip, panty, hose, pearl necklace and earrings, bouquet, silver heels. Circa 1963, #1755.

345. Brenda Starr
12". Seven-piece body having vinyl arms, red rooted wig, tagged lace chemise, heels. Circa 1964, #900, with original box but marked for #915.

346. Shari Lewis
14". Five-piece body having vinyl arms, styled reddish-brown wig, green eyes, tagged rayon jersey blouse, satin skirt, gold belt, slip, panty, hose, pearl earrings, beaded necklace, green straw hat with flowers, green heels. Circa 1959, #1433, with original box and wrist tag. Hard to find in this smaller size.

347. That Girl-Marlo
17". Five-piece body having vinyl arms and head, black eyes, rooted brown hair, tagged red velvet dress, slip, panty, hose, matching red shoes, beaded necklace, solitaire ring. Circa 1967, #1793, with wrist tag.

348. Melinda
14". Five-piece body, rooted brunette wig, open mouth with molded teeth, tagged dress with velvet bodice, organdy sleeves and skirt with lace ruffles, stiff slip, panty, straw hat with ribbon and flowers, anklets, red shoes. Circa 1963, #1415. With hard-to-find brunette hair.

349. Maggie Mixup
17". Eleven-piece body having jointed ankles and vinyl arms, Elise head with freckles, red wig, green eyes, tagged blouse with turquoise checked jumper, slip, black tights, straw hat, heart necklace, cream slippers with bows. Circa 1960, #1812 in box for #1850, original wrist tag.

The following Portrait Series was created in 1966 using the newly-introduced 21" Coco mold. Called the "jewel in the crown" of the Alexander firm, it used a four-piece body mold having the lower legs stationary with one being bent. The face was, of course, created especially for this body to supposedly represent Coco Chanel. They all have exaggerated eyeliner and lash painting, blue shadow, painted nails, and just a hint of a smile. The portraits were released for this one year only and were never used again. They remain amongst the most desirable and sought-after of the Alexander line.

350. Coco Madame Doll
Blonde rooted and styled wig, tagged pink brocade gown with lace and satin ribbon and bow accents, mop cap, full stiff petticoat, pantaloons, white hose, pearl earrings, solitaire ring, black flats. #2060.

351. Renoir Coco
Reddish-blonde rooted and styled wig, tagged blue taffeta gown, matching jacket with black braid and lace trim, matching bonnet with tulle and flowers, stiff petticoat, panty, hose, solitaire ring and earrings, black flats. #2062, with wrist tag.

352. Lissy Coco
Reddish-blonde rooted and styled wig, tagged pink pleated tulle gown with lace covered bodice and peplum? with sequin, pearl, floral, and satin bow accents, organdy liner, stiff petticoat, brilliant earrings, bracelet and tiara, solitaire ring, hose, panty, cream bow flats. #2051.

353. Godey Coco
Blonde rooted and styled wig, tagged red taffeta gown with black lace neckline, velvet jacket with matching lace, ornate velvet hat with tulle, roses and trim, stiff petticoat, solitaire ring, panty, hose, red flats. #2063.

354. Scarlet Coco
Brunette rooted and styled wig, tagged tulle gown with lace bodice, sleeve caps and wide hem, pearl neckline, satin waist sash with rose cluster and roses at hem, horsehair picture hat with flowers and ribbon, stiff petticoat, solitaire ring and earrings, panty, hose, cream flats with red bow. #2061.

355. Blue Melanie Coco
Blonde rooted wig styled in braids and wrapped around head with curls and flowers, tagged blue taffeta gown with lace panels to the sides of front pleats, lace bodice and sleeve accents, velvet bows, stiff petticoat, cameo necklace, solitaire ring, panty, hose, cream flats with rhinestone medallions. #2050.

The following toddlers all use the 12" Janie body having vinyl arms and head and hard plastic torso and chubby toddler legs. They all have rooted hair and innocent expressions to their wide faces.

357. Lucinda
Auburn hair, tagged blue taffeta gown with wide collar, cuffs and hem, pink bows, straw hat with elaborate ribbonwork and plume, slip and pantaloon with blue satin threading, white hose, pink high button shoes, floral parasol. Circa 1969, #1135, with wrist tag.

358. Janie Ballerina
Blonde hair with top curl and flowers, tagged pink tulle and satin tutu with sequins and rhinestone accents, cream ballet slippers. Circa 1965, #1124, with box.

359. Janie Day Dress
Blonde hair with top curl and ribbon, tagged pink cotton dress with rose applique and lace sleeves and collar, slip, panty, anklets, tan shoes. Circa 1964, #1170, with wrist tag.

360. Suzy
Brunette hair, tagged gingham dress with floral pinafore, matching panty, straw hat with matching ribbon and flowers, cotton hose, white shoes, flower basket. Circa 1970, #1150, in original box with wrist tag.

361. Janie Toddler
Blonde hair with top curl and ribbon, tagged white organdy dress with floral embroidery at bodice, panty, anklets, cream shoes. Circa 1964, #1156, in original box with wrist tag.

362. Janie in School
Blonde hair with top curl and ribbon, tagged pique cotton dress with red sleeves and collar accents, matching panty, pencil on cord and arithmetic book, anklets, cream shoes. Circa 1964, #1157, in original box with tag.

363. Smarty
12". Same body as Janie but with different face, rooted red hair, tagged shirt, sweater, shorts, holds arithmetic and first reader books with strap, anklets and tie shoes. Circa 1964, #1150, with box and tag.

364. Mary Ellen Playmate
17". Five-piece bendable vinyl body, Polly face, rooted blonde hair with bow, tagged blue polka dotted dress with striped sash and ruffle, petticoat, panty, hose, matching shoes. Circa 1965, an exclusive doll bought at Marshall Field but also found at Wanamakers.

365. Mary Ellen Playmate
17". Body as previously described, rooted brunette wig with removable twisted chignon, black eyes, tagged organdy gown with lace neckline and tiers, flowers at waist with satin sash, slip, panty, hose, pink shoes. Circa 1965, with wrist tag that notes her as an exclusive. The doll was purchased at Marshall Field.

366. Polly in Original Fashion
17". Body as previously described, brunette rooted wig with removable twisted chignon and flowers, black eyes, dress of lace and floral trimmed blouse, turquoise skirt with same accents, panty, hose, pink heels. Circa 1965, an original dress designed and made by Halina's Doll Fashions of Chicago. She often made fashions for trunk ensembles or store specials.

367. Southern Belle Portrait
21". Seven-piece body having vinyl one-piece arms, rooted and styled blonde wig, Jacqueline face with blue shadow, tagged organdy gown with green satin threaded ribbon, rose at waist, matching hat with roses, lace neckline trim and accents, pleated bottom, cameo necklace, pearl drop earrings, solitaire ring, stiff slip, panty, hose, green heels. Circa 1967, #2170.

368. Scarlett Portrait
21". Seven-piece body having vinyl one-piece arms, rooted and styled brunette wig, Jacqueline face with blue shadow over green eyes, tagged floral print gown with lace accents, threaded satin ribbon trim, velvet waist sash, organdy pleated bottom, straw picture hat with velvet ribbons, cameo necklace, solitaire ring, attached cotton liner, net petticoat, panty, hose, green heels. Circa 1968, #2180, with parasol.

The following dolls are all 21" portraits using the Jacqueline mold. These dolls were displayed by Marshall Field in Chicago in different departments for various events and seasons. All of the clothing is tagged "Halina's Doll Fashions/Chicago" who designed and created the fashions. These outfits were also used when the store created Christmas specials or exclusives which would usually consist of a doll with a wardrobe of different clothing and accessories. They would use a combination of Alexander items as well as those done by this designer to fill out the trunk. Smaller Alexander dolls have also been found with this label in the clothing and these fashions have also been found on dolls purchased at Wanamakers, Vincents and Neiman Marcus. The quality is first-rate and the designs are quite imaginative. They appear in store catalogues from 1961-1966.

369. Lilac Lingerie
Blonde rooted hair, tagged nylon nightie and peignoir with floral appliques, hose, black heels.

370. Mod Chiffon
Blonde rooted hair, tagged multi-colored chiffon float dress with ruffled neckline and hem, taffeta liner, panty, hose, turquoise heels.

371. Mother of the Bride
Brunette rooted Mimi style wig, tagged golden gown with lace top and flowers at the waist, matching headpiece, pearl earrings, lacy short slip, panty, hose and gold heels.

372. Here Comes the Bride
Brunette rooted wig, tagged taffeta straight gown with lace overlay at top and hem, attached matching back piece, tulle veil attached to sequin crown, panty, hose, cream heels and bouquet.

373. Always a Bridesmaid
Brunette rooted wig, tagged pale pink chiffon straight gown with taffeta liner, bright pink chiffon bows at shoulders and attached draping backpiece, ruffled headpiece, panty, hose, cream heels and bouquet. Also included is smaller Royal doll flowergirl in matching outfit with basket of posies.

374. Suzanne
Blonde rooted wig, tagged red nylon gown with gathered bust, rhinestone straps and starbursts on gown, attached liner and red net slip, mink stole, panty, hose, and red heels. Offered in Field's 1967 catalog as Suzanne with a designer wardrobe in a Louis Vuitton trunk for $200.

375. Margot
Brunette rooted upswept wig, tagged pale pink nylon gown with sequined top and streamers down the front, matching purse, scarlett velvet coat with rhinestone buttons, tiara, net slip, panty, hose, silver heels. Offered in Field's 1966 catalogue as Margot with wardrobe in a 24" Louis Vuitton trunk for $200. The trunk from that year had a mink stole and hat and the lingerie and gold suit outfits pictured in this volume.

376. Dinner at Eight
Brunette rooted wig, tagged gold jacket with covered button over matching sheath dress, a matching purse, hose, black heels.

377. Manet Portrait
Brunette rooted and styled wig, tagged red gown with woven gold and silver floral pattern, matching hat with plumes, attached net slip, pearl necklace and bracelets, panty, hose, cream heels. Also said to have been released as an exclusive 1968 Marshall Field Manet Portrait.

378. Peter Pan Characters
Set of the four various-sized characters - Peter, Wendy, Michael and Tinkerbell, as shown, with original boxes and wrist tags. Circa 1969, offered in conjunction with the release of the Walt Disney Movie the same year.

379. Set of Little Women
Group of five 8" dolls as shown from the Little Women series of 1963, #781. All having boxes and wrist tags as shown.

380. Grandma Jane
14". Five-piece body, rooted blonde and blueish hair, tagged blue sheath dress and matching coat, wire glasses, pearl necklace, earrings, slip, panty, hose, purse, and tan flats. Circa 1970, #1420, with original box and tag.

381. Madame Doll
14". Five-piece body, rooted frosted blonde curls, tagged pink brocade gown with lace ruffles and accents, bows, matching mop cap, slip with hidden pocket, pantaloons, white hose, black flats. Circa 1969, #1460, with original box and tag.

382. Jenny Lind
14". Five-piece body, rooted blonde hair with ribbon, tagged floral print dress with velvet bodice trim, white apron, petticoat, panty, white hose, black flats. Circa 1969, #1470, in original box with tag and mohair cat.

383. Sound of Music Set
Group of seven dolls of various sizes and molds from the Sound of Music set. Tagged alpine outfits as shown from the 1971 set with original boxes in smaller, desirable size.

384. Elise Formal
16 1/2". Eleven-piece body having jointed ankles and bendable vinyl arms, blonde styled wig with flowers, tagged cream and silver brocade strapless gown, opera coat of rose satin, pearl drop solitaire earrings, brocade purse, stiff full slip, panty, hose, silver heels. Circa 1963, #1775.

385. The Enchanted Doll
8". Five-piece body, brunette curled wig, tagged pink gingham dress with lace-trimmed pinafore, matching bonnet, slip, pantaloon, white hose, parasol, black shoes. Circa 1980, #281, from a limited edition of 3000 made for The Enchanted Doll House, with box, tags and certificate.

386. The Enchanted Doll
10". Seven-piece body Portrette with brunette wig, tagged outfit as pictured with parasol. Circa 1988, #1558, of a limited edition of 5000 for the 25th Anniversary of The Enchanted Doll House with box, tag and certificate.

387. The Enchanted Doll
8". Five-piece body, brunette wig, another tagged outfit variation as shown. Circa 1981, #1947, from a limited edition of 3,423 made for The Enchanted Doll House with box, tags and certificate.

388. Spanish Boy
8". Seven-piece body, brunette wig, tagged outfit as shown. Circa 1964-68, #779, with wrist tag.

389. Spanish Girl
8". Seven-piece walker body, brunette wig, tagged outfit as shown. Circa 1961-72, #795, with wrist tag.

390. Dutch Boy
8". Seven-piece walker body, cut blonde wig, tagged outfit as shown. Circa 1964-72, #777, with wrist tag.

391. Dutch Girl
8". Seven-piece walker body with Maggie face, green eyes, braided blonde wig, tagged outfit as shown. Circa 1965, #791, with wrist tag.

392. Tyrolean Boy
8". Seven-piece walker body, blonde wig, tagged outfit as shown. Circa 1962, #399, with original box and gold wrist tag.

393. Tyrolean Girl
8". Seven-piece walker body, blonde braided wig, tagged outfit as shown. Circa 1962, #398.

394. French
8". Seven-piece walker body, brunette wig, tagged outfit as shown. Circa 1962, #398, with gold wrist tag.

395. Swedish
8". Seven-piece walker body, blonde wig, tagged outfit as shown. Circa 1961, #492, with original box and gold wrist tag.

Left to right: Top to Bottom

396. Bolivia
8". Seven-piece walker body, braided brunette wig, tagged outfit as shown. Circa 1963-66, #386, with wrist tag.

397. Argentina Girl
8". Seven-piece body, braided brunette wig, tagged outfit as shown. Circa 1965-72, #771.

398. Mexican
8". Seven-piece body, brunette wig braided in back, tagged outfit as shown. Circa 1964-72, #776, in original box with wrist booklet.

399. Portugal
8". Seven-piece body, brunette wig, tagged outfit as shown. Circa 1968-72, #785, in original box with wrist booklet.

400. Brazil
8". Seven-piece walker body, brunette wig, tagged outfit as shown. Circa 1965, #773, with wrist booklet.

401. Argentina Boy
8". Seven-piece walker body, short brunette wig, tagged outfit as shown. Circa 1965-66, #772.

402. Peruvian Boy
8". Seven-piece body, short brunette wig, tagged outfit as shown. Circa 1965-66, #770.

403. Ecuador
8". Seven-piece walker body, braided brunette wig, tagged outfit as shown. Circa 1965, #787.

404. Indonesia
8". Seven-piece brown body with Maggie face, tagged ceremonial costume as shown. Circa 1970, #779, in original box with wrist booklet.

405. Korea
8". Seven-piece brown body with Maggie face, tagged ceremonial costume as shown. Circa 1968, #772, with original box and wrist booklet.

406. Vietnam
8". Seven-piece brown body with Maggie face, tagged outfit as shown. Circa 1968-69, #788, in original box with wrist booklet.

407. Japan
8". Seven-piece brown body with Maggie face, tagged outfit as shown. Circa 1968-72, #770.

408. Polish
8". Seven-piece body, blonde braided wig, tagged outfit as shown. Circa 1964-72, #780, with box and wrist booklet.

409. Hungarian
8". Seven-piece walker body, blonde braided wig, tagged outfit as shown with metal headpiece. Circa 1963-78, #797, with wrist booklet.

410. Rumania
8". Seven-piece body, brunette wig in back braid, tagged outfit as shown. Circa 1968-72, #786, in original box with wrist booklet.

411. Czech
8". Seven-piece body, brunette wig, tagged outfit as shown. Circa 1972, #764.

412. Russian
8". Seven-piece walker body, braided brunette wig, tagged outfit as shown. Circa 1968-72, #0774, in original box with wrist booklet.

The following Portraits show the variation in design and creativity of the Alexander firm. They all use the Jacqueline face with blue shadow and expressive eyes and have seven-piece bodies with one-piece vinyl arms unless otherwise noted. The wigs are all rooted and highly styled in curls and falls.

414. Godey Portrait
21". Blonde wig, tagged red velvet strapless gown with overcoat of matching fabric with elaborate black braid and buttons, lace short mitts, black straw hat with ribbon and net veil, red stone necklace, jeweled earrings, solitaire ring, stiff slip, pantaloon, hose, red heels. Circa 1969, #2195, with wrist tag.

415. Mimi Portrait
21". Blonde wig, tagged white taffeta gown with square neck and elaborate pink floss braiding on front, rose taffeta opera coat with tulle and floral wrap, matching hat, solitaire earrings, necklace and ring, stiff slip, pantaloons, hose, pink heels. Circa 1971, #2170, with wrist tag. Offered only this year.

416. Queen Portrait
21". Dark blonde wig, tagged white brocade gown with silver threads, red and blue ribbon sash with accents, mitts, tiara, brilliant earrings, bracelets and ring, pearl necklace, stiff slip, panty, hose, cream heels. Circa 1968, #2185.

417. Bride Portrait
21". Blonde wig, tagged gown with lace overlay, sequined neckline and waist and tulle bottom pleats, veil attached to floral headpiece, pearl necklace and earrings, solitaire ring, bouquet, stiff slip, pantaloons, white heels. Circa 1969, #2192, with wrist tag.

418. Jenny Lind
14". Five-piece body, blonde styled wig, tagged pink slipper satin gown with lace accents and ribbon flower accents, brilliant earrings, stiff petticoat, pantaloons, pink flats. Circa 1970, #1491, with wrist tag.

419. Jenny Lind Portrait
21". Blonde styled wig, tagged pink slipper satin gown with lace edges and flower at neckline, brilliant earrings, solitaire ring, bouquet of roses, stiff petticoat, pantaloons, pink heels. Circa 1969, #2191, with wrist tag.

420. Gainsborough Portrait

21". Reddish-blonde wig, tagged blue scalloped taffeta gown with ecru lace overlay, pleated tulle underskirt, lace sleeves, rosebud accents, satin back bow, tulle hat with rose clusters, solitaire ring, stiff petticoat, pantaloons, blue heels. Circa 1973, #2192, with wrist tag.

421. Agatha Portrait

21". Reddish-brown wig, tagged lavender taffeta gown with scalloped edges, pleated underskirt, trimmed with braid and flowers, velvet waist sash, horsehair picture hat with flowers, cameo necklace, pearl waist pin, solitaire ring, stiff petticoat, pantaloons, purple heels. Circa 1979, #2230, with wrist tag and original box.

422. Gainsborough Portrait

21". Reddish-brown wig, tagged pink taffeta gown with ecru lace overlay, waist sash with large bustled back bow, pink horsehair hat with ribbon and flowers, cameo necklace, solitaire ring, stiff petticoat, pantaloons, pink heels. Circa 1978, #2211, with wrist tag and original box.

423. Scarlett Portrait
21". Brunette wig, green eyes, tagged green taffeta gown, matching braided jacket with lace cuffs, matching bonnet with feathered edges, cameo necklace, solitaire ring, stiff petticoat and pantaloons with threaded ribbon, black heels. Circa 1975, #2292, with wrist tag in original box.

424. Cornelia Portrait
21". Blonde wig, tagged pink taffeta gown with white braided front, matching opera coat with tulle wrap, matching hat with flower, solitaire ring, stiff petticoat, pantaloons, pink heels. Circa 1972, #2191, with wrist tag and box.

425. Scarlett Portrait
21". Brunette curled wig, green eyes, tagged rosebud printed satin gown with threaded satin ribbon and lace bodice, satin sash with back bow, straw picture hat with flowers and ribbon, green solitaire necklace, solitaire ring, stiff petticoat, pantaloons, parasol, pink heels. Circa 1976, #2210, with wrist tag, in original box.

426. Cornelia Portrait
21". Blonde wig, tagged blue taffeta gown with square neckline, matching opera coat with gold and blue trim, tulle hat with flowers, solitaire ring, pearl-drop necklace, stiff petticoat, pantaloons, silver heels. Circa 1976, #2212, in original box with wrist tag and Filene's price tag.

427. Agatha Portrait
21". Reddish-brown wig, tagged turquoise taffeta gown with pleated underskirt, floral and ribbon accents, pink horsehair picture hat with flowers, cameo necklace, pearl pin and solitaire ring, stiff petticoat, pantaloons, silver blue heels. Circa 1981, #2230, with wrist tag and box.

428. Magnolia Portrait
21". Reddish-brown wig, tagged pink taffeta dress with ruffled skirt front tiers, flowers at waist and on ruffles, matching horsehair picture hat with flowers, moonstone-type necklace, solitaire ring, stiff petticoat, pantaloons, pink heels. Circa 1977, #2297, with wrist tag and box.

429. Marie Antoinette Portrait
21". Blonde highly-styled wig having ribbon and plume, tagged floral-print satin gown with pink taffeta front insert covered with gold and white lace, tulle and lace accents, sequin braiding and satin bows, triple pearl necklace, brilliant pin, solitaire ring, fan, stiff petticoat, pantaloons, pink heels. Circa 1987-88, #2248, with original box and wrist tag.

430. Scarlett Portrait
21". Brunette wig with ribbons, green eyes, tagged rose print satin gown with lace bodice ruffles and ribbon threading, velvet sash, straw picture hat with flowers, solitaire ring, parasol, stiff petticoat, pantaloons, green heels. Circa 1986 only, #2255, with original box and wrist tag.

431. Scarlett Portrait
21". Brunette wig, green eyes, tagged white cotton tiered gown with lace edges and ruffled bodice, green velvet sash, jeweled pin, green solitaire ring, bouquet of flowers, stiff petticoat, pantaloons, green heels. Circa 1987-88, #2247, with original box and wrist tag.

432. Mary Queen of Scots Portrait

21". Brunette braided wig, tagged elaborate gown with gold satin sleeves, attached burgundy velvet jumper and golden embellished overgarment overall, lace cuffs, pleated tulle neck ruff, matching headpiece with braid, pearls and jewels, two heavy golden necklaces, green and red solitaire rings, lace handkerchief, stiff petticoat, pantaloons and special golden heels. Circa 1988-89, #2252, with original box and wrist tag.

433. Toulouse Lautrec Portrait

21". Red wig, tagged pink and black striped slipper satin gown with pink underskirt, fringed front with lace bodice insert, lace mitts, feather boa, reticule, black straw hat with plume, cameo pin, solitaire ring, stiff petticoat, pantaloons, black heels. Circa 1986-87, #2250, with original box and wrist tag.

434. Sarah Bernhardt Portrait

21". Blonde wig, tagged cocoa velvet gown with matching jacket both having braidwork, lace jabot and sleeve cuffs, matching hat with ribbons and veil, cameo pin, solitaire ring, stiff petticoat, panty, brown heels. Circa 1987, #2249, with original box and wrist tag.

Two Very Special Portraits of the Madame Herself -

435. Pink Madame Alexander Portrait
21". Body as previously described but with a special face created for this doll only, blonde styled wig with velvet ribbon, tagged pink slipper satin gown with rhinestones at waist, chiffon wrap with gold and jeweled accents, rose corsage, brilliant earrings, bracelet and solitaire ring, sequin purse, stiff petticoat, lace panty, gold heels. Circa 1985-87, #2290, in original box with special wrist tag.

436. Blue Madame Alexander Portrait
21". Body as previously described but with special face created for this doll only, blonde styled wig, tagged blue taffeta gown with silver floral net overlay and rhinestone accented hem, tulle wrap with flower, taffeta sash, tiara, jeweled necklace, solitaire ring, bracelet, silver purse, stiff petticoat, lace panty, special silver lame heels with bows. Circa 1988-90, #2295, with original box and special wrist tag.